You Can't Sleep Through Your Awakening

By Jane Simmons

The Q Effect, LLC
www.theqeffect.com

Jane Simmons' books are available for order through
The Q Effect, LLC

Visit The Q Effect website at www.theqeffect.com

Printed in the United States of America

First Printing: March 2017
Published by The Q Effect Publishing, LLC

ISBN: 978-1-62747-401-6
eBook ISBN: 978-1-62747-432-0

I have tried to recreate personal stories from my memories
of them. Some names and identifying details have been
changed to protect the privacy of individuals.

Some portions of this book have appeared in the
author's earlier works.

Dedicated to the Bright Lights who are my
beloved grandchildren:

Bree-Ann, Julian, Mason, Liam and Alexander

Planet Earth is a way better place because you are here.

May all beings find joy and freedom on life's journey
of self-discovery.

Contents

Introduction

In the iconic movie, *The Matrix,* the hero Neo is asked to choose to either wake up or to continue living unconsciously. He is offered a red pill that will open his eyes to the truth that he is living a life imprisoned by his own mind, or a blue pill that will let him return to unconscious living. He is forewarned that if he chooses the red pill to awaken, there would be no turning back. Neo decides to take the red pill – and his life is never the same.

To be asleep is to be unaware of one's true authentic nature. That deeper essence can be covered up by anxiety, stress, regret, resentment, shame, guilt, any or all of the above. As a result, the innate aliveness underlying it all is completely overlooked.

Without realizing it, much of humanity has been experiencing life through a filtered lens of beliefs, perceptions and assumptions largely taken on during childhood, through family, friends and cultural influence. This conditioned form of unconscious "waking sleep" is the definition of "blue pill living."

The poet, Stanley Kuntz advises us to, "Live in the layers, not on the litter." Red-pill living has the potential of opening our eyes to any littering of unconscious cultural/social programming that is currently underground, and yet running the show. Awakening brings forth a moment of clarity, insight and understanding, which can cut through the conditioning and reveal a deeper truth that lives within the layers.

Sometimes those awakenings can be rather rude.

A blinding red pill moment shocked me into action during a memorial service for a teenager who had taken his own life.

Hundreds attended his memorial, and the personal sharing of stories, memories and common history lasted well over an hour. As I listened, I caught a glimpse of his magnificent soul and the depth of love that poured out from family and friends alike. Was he able to let in the love that others had for him? If he had known that he was *this* loved, *this* valued, would he have made a different choice?

The answer can only be a qualified maybe. But this experience served to whirl me around in my tracks and ignite a fire under me.

This book is a result of the lighting of that fire. A combination of personal memoir, shared stories, psychological study, scientific learning and spiritual discourse, the book explores what it actually means to wake up. It shines a light on unconscious living and provides tools that can assist in the awakening process. But as the author Sam Harris points out, "There is barely enough time in a book – or in a life – to get to the point."

For that reason, the book's focus is narrowed to four arenas. You will learn simple practices using the *FACE* Formula which consists of Forgiveness, Appreciation, Compassion and Embodiment that will allow you to "face" whatever is showing up in your world in an awakened and present state of being. In this healing form of conscious awareness, you can now unmask the Face of the Authentic Self within you, and see it mirrored back from every pair of eyes. In addition, throughout the book, you will find "Red Pill Practice" questions and exercises to help put these principles into effect.

There is a spectrum of ways to wake up the sleepwalking self, ranging from gentle chimes on one end of the continuum to screeching alarm clocks on the other. But no matter how the awakening occurs, one thing remains constant. You just can't sleep through it. It takes an intention of choosing to pay attention, deliberately deciding to take the red pill and making the conscious choice to stay awake.

The red pill of awareness is always being offered to us, moment by moment, situation by situation, and conversation by conversation. So the question is: "Will you take the red pill or the blue pill?" The choice is yours and the moment is now. If you are yearning to live an awakened life, free of being run by largely unconscious programming, please read on.

Chapter 1 From Seeing to Being

"The mind, once stretched by a new idea, never returns to its original dimensions." Ralph Waldo Emerson

At the risk of stating the obvious, you can't sleep through your awakening. Trust me, I've tried. As the Armenian spiritual teacher, Georges Gurdjieff, is quoted as saying, "You cannot unconsciously become conscious."

It seems fairly evident that you have to wake up in order to live an awakened life. Yet the issue appears to be that we, as a species, are unaware of even being asleep.

There is a story told of Siddhartha Gautama, who reached enlightenment under the Bodhi tree after forty-five days of contemplation in the Silence, and became known as the Buddha (meaning The Enlightened One).

A curious group of townspeople gathered and asked him, "Are you a god?"

He answered, "No."

Then they inquired, "Are you a man?"

Again, he responded, "No."

"An angel?" He shook his head.

Puzzled, they questioned him once more, "If you are not a god, you're not a man, and you are not an angel, what are you?"

He replied, "I am awake."

This well-known Buddhist tale illustrates so beautifully the potential for transformation that comes from an experience of awakening, as well as the depth of spiritual understanding it engenders. As we wake up, we sense our connection with something greater, our eyes are opened through a flash of insight and suddenly there is the dawning on our awareness of something previously hidden from us. It can come in the form of a blinding "aha" moment. One such moment for me occurred in my early years.

Angels, Skipping Ropes and Cartoons

It was a beautiful summer afternoon with the sun shining brightly, and I was sitting cross-legged in the backyard of my six-and-a-half-year-old best friend's home. We were having a serious, pint-sized version of a metaphysical conversation, when the discussion turned to what happened after death.

As we pondered the possibilities, my friend declared, her eyes shining with excitement, "Heaven is a place where you are happy forever and you just float around all the time on top of the clouds with the angels." I could see by her face that she relished the thought, but frankly it didn't appeal to me at all. In fact, the image of just floating on a cloud forever filled my adventurous soul with a feeling of dread. My heart turned to lead.

Don't get me wrong; I liked angels well enough. I hadn't met any in person, but the ones I'd heard about seemed pretty cool. They were always bringing good news. But floating around with one on a cloud for eternity? What would happen to all the fun things in life like skipping rope and playing baseball? Splashing through mud puddles in new rain boots? What about warm, sandy beaches to play on, frolicking with friends in the water and building sandcastles? Were there any sleds or toboggans on top of those clouds? No more rainbows, carnivals, Christmas mornings or celebrating birthdays? And most importantly, what would I do without Saturday morning cartoons?

Eternal repose on an endless sea of white with an angel did not sound like much fun. In fact it sounded, well... to be honest...

Before I could censor them, the words spilled out. "That would be so boring!"

Oh, great.

In just five short words, I had effectively insulted the entire heavenly host by inferring that they were all too dull for me to hang out with. My blasphemous words hung in the air as my friend's excitement turned to fear. She gasped in horror, sliding away from me and searching the heavens, as if waiting for the sky to begin falling or at least maybe for a lightning bolt to strike me.

With no such sign from above, she slowly regained her composure, then wondered aloud if perhaps I would prefer the alternative. I considered the possibility of spending an eternity in hell and assumed that I had probably just secured my spot, courtesy of the angel insult. Turning to my friend, I asked, "So, if I do something wrong, God is going to punish me FOREVER? I am going to be sent to a place where I am going to burn and be tortured and never escape? Never? *EVER?*"

The heavy feeling of dread deepened as I imagined such a gruesome prospect. I realized that even in the half-dozen years of my short life span, I had probably reached my quota of bad deeds, and consequently, my fate seemed to already be sealed. Was there no hope? My friend's solemn silence told me that she didn't think there was.

As I sat there thinking about how wrong this all seemed, a lightning bolt *did* actually appear. Only it wasn't in the sky, it was in my mind. In fact, every cell of my body lit up with understanding and excitement as I was suddenly seized with an undeniable, indisputable, unshakable knowingness that told me without a shadow of a doubt that there was no such place as hell.

Hell. Was. Not. Real.

The story I had been fed about an eternal afterlife of torture was not the truth. As the light dawned within me, a feeling of warmth and peace enveloped me. It was much like awakening from a frightful nightmare and being snuggled in your mother's arms, feeling deeply loved, and grateful to discover that it had all just been a dream. With great assurance, total relief and no fear this time of speaking it out loud, I boldly proclaimed the truth to the universe and anyone else within earshot, including my still-rather-shaken friend, "The God that *I* know would *never* do that to me."

The loving, compassionate Presence that I had felt within me, my deepest and dearest friend, would never consign me to an eternity of suffering. But wait, there was more! God would not ever sentence me to a colorless existence of eternal boredom either. No, the reality of it was that the loving Presence that I felt within my heart would welcome me with open arms and offer the grand prize of eternal, never-ending joy.

And probably cartoons.

The depth of conviction that had suddenly emerged from me came from a much deeper place of understanding than just my conscious mind. It was a knowingness beyond doubt, one that came from a heartfelt experience rather than a mere thought.

Once you catch a glimpse of something that lies beyond what the cultural belief might assume, there is no turning back. The mind is stretched and it never quite returns back to its former size.

In that moment, at the tender age of six and a half, I had my first experience of an awakening moment. But it would not, by any stretch, be the last.

From Skipping Rope to Boxing Ring

Fast-forward a few decades to a time of life when I found myself at a crossroads, stumbling around in an inner wilderness of confusion, searching for clarity around my life's purpose. I decided to take a plunge and embark on a solitary, native-style vision quest as a possible avenue to gain that clarity. For three days I camped on the land, deep in the forest, sleeping in a tent, fasting, while miles away from showers, kitchens or any indoor plumbing.

My small space was bordered by rows of colorful prayer flags, hanging from a rope and wound around the trees that surrounded the area. I thought how much it looked like a boxing ring! The thought actually appealed to me in some odd way, giving me strength to get through the difficulties that came with fasting in isolation. I could almost hear the theme from *Rocky* as I stood in the center of the "ring" and began my quest. It was challenging, yet exhilarating.

I spent the daylight hours within the "ring" in the midst of forested beauty, focusing on my breathing as I sat in silence, immersed in the beautiful sounds of nature. At night, as I lay sleeping in my tent, I awoke every couple of hours, remembering vivid, incredible dreams. One in particular introduced me to a native guide who appeared, and led me to a file cabinet, where together we opened the drawer to peer into old, ancient, dusty files and then cleared them out. It was a liberating dream, and I awoke from it feeling excited, refreshed, clearer, lighter. As I contemplated the meaning of it, I realized that during the entire vision-quest process, I had been clearing out some of my past that had been "filed away" for years. This dawning realization seemed to serve as the threshold for the amazing experience that was about to unfold.

As I stepped out of my tent, still immersed in the feeling of lightness and freedom from the dream, I heard the sound of a woodpecker in a nearby tree. I zeroed in on it as I followed an unmistakable urge to locate the bird visually while continuing to listen. The combination of watching and hearing the bird resulted in an almost hypnotic effect. As I continued to stare, the experience I had could be likened to peering at a design with a 3-D image hidden within it. Then with a change in ocular perspective, a softening of the eyes, having the picture "magically" appear in the midst of the design.

By shifting the focus of my perception, suddenly the entire scene changed. Right before my eyes, the whole forest "morphed" into pure energy. Peeling back a veneer of visibility, the outer forms faded and then fell away. In that startling moment, the pure energy behind all matter was clearly revealed. Everything was vibrating with the essence of sheer aliveness. The level of well-being that flooded my body lifted me to a greater vision and the illusory feeling of "I" fell away.

This was the heaven that my six-year-old self had glimpsed. It was even better than cartoons!

Ever-increasing joy exploded from within my heart, filling my body and mind. As I gazed in open-mouthed astonishment, I experienced the One Life that animates everything – and I found myself sinking to my knees, almost dizzy with awe and gratitude that I had been given this gift.

The quantum concept of the wave and the particle - energy and matter - suddenly made perfect sense to me. I realized that everything and everyone was localized Spirit in physical form, both the wave *and* the particle.

At that point, I swear, the *Rocky* theme started up again.

Although there was a gargantuan gulf between this experience and my childhood awakening in terms of depth of intensity, spiritual maturity and understanding, one thing remained constant – seeing beyond appearances to a deeper reality. That is the common denominator that awakening experiences share. You wake up to something you hadn't seen before.

But it's not enough just to see it.

Although both of these moments provided exciting insights that opened up my awareness to something much greater than I had previously known, there was a third experience that connected all of the dots and propelled me into action.

Don't Postpone Joy

I stood at the podium and looked out at the hundreds of pairs of eyes, all of them waiting expectantly. My role for the next two hours was to facilitate a memorial service for a teenage boy who had, only one week previously, ended his own life.

By all appearances, this young man had everything to live for with a bright future ahead of him. He had just graduated from high school, had a good summer job lined up and college was beckoning.

He was surrounded by a loving family and had lots of friends. They described him as someone who had a great love of music, classic books and stand-up comedy. He was known for his sparkling wit, intelligence and delightfully endearing quirkiness. And yet, one evening he ended it all with a loaded gun.

It was, without a doubt, the most difficult memorial I have ever done. In the days leading up to it, as I prepared for the service, I went over all of the flowery words, readings and prayers that I would typically say. Close to ninety percent of it was tossed out. There needed to be a lot more time allotted to inviting family and friends to share their stories, their histories and their grief.

The family had estimated that there might be around a hundred people coming but over three hundred showed up. One by one they came forward, young and old, family and friends. On and on the sharing continued, well into the afternoon, and as it did, I caught a glimpse of a creative, fun-loving, caring, intelligent, humorous, sweet soul who was deeply loved.

It was standing room only and the sharing of the stories was a giant tribute to this young man. I was deeply shaken by the experience, especially hearing his grandmother speak about the special bond she'd had with him. I could so strongly relate to that.

And as I listened, I wondered.

I wondered if he really knew how much he was loved and valued. Was he able to let in that love? Did he ever see the beautiful gifts within him, as everyone else had? Was there a depth of mental and emotional pain hidden within him that led him to take his own life? If he could have escaped that inner suffering and had known his own value and worth, would he have made a different choice?

I'll never know the answer to those questions. But I do know this. On that day, a fire was ignited under me, and it quickly grew into a bonfire within my heart. Fanning those flames was the realization that although at a very young age, I had dismissed the afterlife version of hell as completely ludicrous, the subsequent decades of living had shown me that it was possible to be imprisoned in a very real *internal* hell in our current life. Suddenly, I was seized with an urgency to step out of that mire of suffering and to help others to do the same.

The resulting emergent impulse generated a transformative shift within me that led to diving fully into my mission in life with a clear understanding that it is not enough to just *see* the light. Transformation is all about learning to *be* the light.

By learning and sharing the art of wholehearted living, we can all open the prison door, awaken to the true authentic self within, discover our own self-worth and stop postponing a joy-filled life. Awakened insight, married with compassionate action, is the key.

Red Pill Practice

1. What is an example of an awakening moment in *your* life? Is it an insight you've received, an intuitive understanding, an experience of Presence, or one that startled you out of a moment of unconscious living?

2. Is there a defining moment that propelled you into some kind of compassionate action?

3. Describe the experience here, along with any insight you received.

Chapter 2 Red Pill, Blue Pill

"Now I do not know whether I was then a man dreaming I was a butterfly, or whether I am now a butterfly, dreaming I am a man." Chang Tzu

In the quintessential movie, *The Matrix,* the main hero Neo meets a mysterious character named Morpheus, who offers him the opportunity to awaken to the awareness that what he believes to be true, solid and real is not at all what it seems. He pulls out two pills, a red pill that if ingested will open Neo's eyes to this truth, and a blue pill that will allow him to go back to sleep, remaining unaware that anything unusual is going on under the surface of apparent reality. Neo wrestles with the decision but finally dives in, making the choice to live consciously. He swallows the red pill and his world is changed forever.

The Matrix is one of my favorite movies because it illustrates, in a very graphic way, not only what it means to awaken to what is real in our lives but also the consequences of staying asleep. It is entirely possible to walk through life unconsciously − seemingly awake, and yet not present either. When our head and our feet are never in the same place, we are not really living at all. We're just going through the motions on autopilot.

The fact is that we do it all the time.

Have you ever been behind the wheel of a car, driving for a distance, and then suddenly realizing that you can't remember a good portion of the ride? The prospect of self-driving cars soon to be arriving on our highways brings up a lot of fear and apprehension. And yet, how many vehicles are *already* being driven robotically by people lost in thought, and effectively asleep at the wheel?

Science Fiction movies abound that illustrate the horror of having robots going rogue, from the insane ramblings of HAL 9000 in *2001: A Space Odyssey* to the seemingly indestructible, programmed-to-kill *Terminator*. What is missing in these scenarios is the guidance of the human heart. The thing about using autopilot on an airplane is that there is still a real, live pilot in the cockpit. Although it assists in keeping the plane on course, autopilot is not a reason for the pilot to abdicate his or her role in controlling the plane.

Unconscious living arises when we vacate the driver's seat.

I remember a time of being despondent about a loved one's troubling medical diagnosis, and driving somewhere while totally oblivious to the outside world. I was startled out of my reverie by a horn beeping and a man giving me a "one finger salute". My first reaction was to salute back, but then I realized that I *needed* to be awakened in that moment. What this told me was that I should either drive in an aware state in the first place or get out from behind the wheel until I could.

When we unconsciously sleepwalk through our days, we relinquish the reins to unconscious programming. Aside from being a danger to ourselves and others, we don't fully experience life. Ultimately, we miss a deeper sense of what is real.

But we don't just sleep*walk*, we sleep-talk, sleep-listen, sleep-eat, sleep-drive, sleep-work, sleep-text. You get the idea. We can go through life never fully present.

The mind is habitually unsatisfied with the present moment, so it might indulge in thinking about the past, stuck in memories of what has been. It may be clutching with longing or immersed in painful regret, mesmerized by the scene in the rear-view mirror.

Our mind might also be involved in what has been called "nexting" – namely, focusing on what is coming just over the horizon. It may be entangled in some imaginary future, and thinking *that* is where fulfillment lies, rather than being fully in the here and now.

This phenomenon is poignantly captured in an anonymous poem that was found on a subway wall:

First I was dying to finish high school and start college.
Then I was dying to finish college and start working.
Then I was dying to marry and have children.

15

*Then I was dying for my children to grow old
enough for school, so I could return to work.
Then I was dying to retire.
Now I am dying and I realize that I forgot to live.*

When I read those words, I asked myself how much I was race-walking through my life, dying to be somewhere else and never being present. Was I skimming the surface? Avoiding the present moment? Missing what was really happening? And most importantly, at the end of my days would I look back, realize that I forgot to live, and feel that same regret?

Wakey Wakey

What does it mean to be awake? Webster defines it as "to cease sleeping" and "to become conscious or aware." Awakening brings forth a moment of clarity, insight and understanding. It can also startle us out of drowsily sleepwalking through life, with the eye-opening result of making the unconscious conscious.

Living this kind of an awakened life is available to us right now. However, it takes some work. Neo needed training to learn how to function in a world that was asleep. He needed to mature in the awakened arena. In the same way, we need to learn to adjust and transition into conscious living.

It may take some commitment, perseverance and education about what is keeping us asleep, but the good

16

news is that we have within us all we need to wake up. We hold the red pill in the palm of our hands.

Not every experience of awakening is of the lightning-bolt variety. There is a spectrum of possibility ranging from the *gentle-motherly-stroking-of-the-hair-and-inviting-you-into-wakefulness* brand to the *rude-ice-water-in-the-face-hey-you-get-up* method. Awakening is not always fun. Wake-up calls can be rude and jarring. Your world seems shattered.

Dr. Paul Ray and Sherry Anderson in their book, *The Cultural Creatives*, describe awakening in this way:

"Waking up can be immediately physical, a quiet deep contact between yourself and everything. It can come as the fruit of a long practice; leaving you melted and grateful. Waking up can be filled with pain; an ice pick between the shoulder blades or a tearing apart in the soft tissues of the heart. You see how you have harmed someone, or betrayed yourself, or failed to speak out against injustice. You recognize poverty, loneliness, grief that you have resolutely walked past for years, or a lifetime."

When I was a teenager, I was once unceremoniously fired from a job and immediately shown the door. That got my attention and it turned my world upside down. Think about times when you were "rudely awakened" – the loss of a loved one, a diagnosis. Where were you when you heard the news that the Twin Towers had come down?

Those experiences have a habit of shattering our complacency, of taking us off autopilot and landing us squarely into the only place we can live an awakened life – the present moment.

However, awakening moments don't have to be that traumatic; they can be much gentler if we decide to use whatever is showing up as the catalyst for our awakening. Being fired, while it certainly felt crushing at the time, ended up being the portal through which major positive change emerged in my world. What if something happening in your life right now had the potential to be the stimulus for your growth, development and transformation? What if it could reveal a deeper Wholeness that is behind all of what you think is real, consequently bringing an empowering aliveness to your conscious awareness?

No matter how the awakening occurs, one thing remains constant. You just can't sleep through it. You cannot unconsciously become conscious. It takes an intention of choosing to pay attention, of deliberately deciding to take the red pill and making the conscious choice to stay awake.

As the Sufi poet Rumi writes,

> *The breeze at dawn has secrets to tell you.*
> *Don't go back to sleep.*
> *You must ask for what you really want.*
> *Don't go back to sleep.*

*People are going back and forth across
the doorsill
Where the two worlds touch.
The door is round and open.
Don't go back to sleep.*

Be forewarned, however. Once you take the red pill, there's no turning back. We can't "unknow" these principles once we have learned them. Although it can be tempting to slip back into unconscious behaviors, the truth is that once our eyes have been opened to "red pill living," we see that living in an unconscious way is not living at all; it is snoozing through our existence and effectively missing our lives.

So, the question on the table is. Are you willing to take the red pill? The time to choose is now. And the decision is yours.

Red Pill Practice

1. Give an example of a moment in your life when something happened that seemed to be a negative experience, but after the passage of time, you were able to find a redeeming gift of some kind within the situation.

2. What happened?

3. What was the gift?

19

Chapter 3 What Exactly is in this Red Pill?

"Embrace each challenge in your life as an opportunity for self-transformation." Bernie Siegel

It's always a good idea to know what is in the medications we take, and what the possible side effects are. Red pill practices are no exception. I am happy to report that the ingredient list is healthy, safe, easy to find and effective. There is no possibility of overdosing and no contraindications. The only side effect is that we stop dragging our past around like a sack of weights.

The ingredients aren't foreign, hard-to-pronounce chemical names. It's easy to remember the components that make up the red pill if we use the letters in the word *FACE*, standing for the transformational practices of Forgiveness, Appreciation, Compassion and Embodiment. In the following chapters we will explore the powerful effect of the Hawaiian self-forgiveness practice of *ho'oponopono,* (okay, maybe *one* ingredient might be hard to pronounce), the incredible results that arise from using self-compassion, the kick-butt generative ability of appreciation and how to be the change we seek through authentic action.

When you forgive, appreciate, feel compassion and embody the practice, you can "face" the experience without resistance or combat, and in so doing, unlock the gifts it brings. Red pill practices also aid in recognizing the previously hidden face of the Authentic Self, the revealing of humanity's true essence of wholeness. It's not enough to read or learn about them, however; we actually need to put what we have learned into practice and use them.

The kinds of spiritual tools available to us to aid in our awakening journey can be loosely classified in two arenas: *translational* and *transformational.* Transformational practices help us to awaken from the dream of unconscious living, while translational ones spruce up the dream a little. They both have merit. But to understand the difference, consider the following scenario:

Imagine that you happen upon a person who is asleep, and who is obviously having a frightening nightmare with arms and legs thrashing about, trying to escape something fearful. Would you:

Choice #1: Fall asleep next to them so you can enter the nightmare, find out what the problem is and help them fight it?

Choice #2: Gently wake them up to let them know they have been dreaming and that what they thought was happening wasn't real?

Choice #2 *does* seem to be the more prudent course of action.

Choice #1 is a translational practice that is trying to improve the dream with a nice, pleasant shoulder massage. Sometimes we just need that. Choice #2 is a transformational spiritual tool that can startle us into seeing that the dream isn't real. It tends to be more like a deep-tissue Shiatsu treatment.

One way to understand the difference between the two is to imagine someone who, after forty years of service, is suddenly losing their job. They are going through a shattering dark night of the soul, devastated because of their longtime association with their workplace identity. A translational approach to this situation would be to use tools like affirmations, treasure mapping and visualization in order to find a new job. A transformational method, while perhaps utilizing those tools, would also include doing some deeper work that explores what is beyond the work identity, using the loss as a means of becoming more conversant with the Authentic Self. One method improves the dream – and the other wakes up from it.

I am reminded of the story of how a mother eagle builds a nest for her eggs. She starts with thorns and sharp, broken branches, then lines the nest with soft feathers. The birds hatch, and as they begin to grow, the nest becomes too small for them and she starts taking out the feathers to make room. Little by little, the thorns and branches come to the surface and the nest becomes too uncomfortable for the young eagles. They finally learn to fly and they leave. The discomfort has the potential to help us grow into who we have come here to be - if we use it to do so.

While red pill practices are definitely on the transformational side of the equation, it isn't that there is anything wrong with translational practices. It all depends on our intention.

And the good news is that it is possible to come up with a hybrid. Let's call it Choice #3: telling the truth with compassion.

Tripping Over the Threshold of a Dream

In the last week of her life, my mother had entered a coma that she was never to emerge from. She was lying in a hospital bed at home, surrounded by family. There was nothing left for us to do except to keep her comfortable and stay by her side.

A different hospice nurse arrived each day to care for her. My family was very grateful for the kind, compassionate and caring professionals who paid close attention to her needs. One day, however, the nurse who showed up seemed rushed, distracted and rather irritated by having to be there.

She went about her work in a humorless fashion, and it wasn't an issue until she gave my mother some medication. As soon as the injection was administered, my mom immediately became very agitated and began to move her arms and legs around, with fear written all over her face. I called for the nurse, who callously waved it off and assured me that my mom was fine and would settle down as soon as the painkiller entered her system.

Only she didn't. She got worse.

Again, I called to the nurse, who frankly appeared to be more interested in filling in forms than caring for my mother. She seemed highly annoyed with my repeated pestering. Finally, I asked her what was in the injection and she replied with an irritated edge to her voice, "It's just a derivative of morphine; she will be fine."

No!

Written right into her medical record, which the nurse had not bothered to read, were the emphatic instructions that under NO CIRCUMSTANCES was my mother EVER to be given ANYTHING with morphine in it, because its only effect in the past was to trap her in endless, horrific, hellish nightmares.

Helplessly, I looked back at my mother, who was definitely immersed in something that was terrifying her. I must confess, it took every ounce of superhuman strength I could muster and many years of martial-arts training to hold back from exploding all over that nurse.

Instead, my daughter and I instantly sprang into action, one stationed at each ear, while we soothingly talked to my mom, tag-team style.

"Mom, I know you are afraid, but you are just having a dream."

"What you're seeing is not real. I know it looks real, but it isn't. You are having a nightmare."

"Grandma, we are here with you right now, and we are not leaving your side. You are safe with us."

"We are staying right here, Mom, and we won't ever leave you."

Over and over we whispered the words as we stroked her hair and held her hand. Finally, we saw her begin to calm down, relief returning to her face. Her breathing slowed down.

Our words got through.

The nightmare ended.

And when it did, she experienced peace. We sent the nurse packing with a request to the agency to never have her return.

My mother was stuck in an illusory state of fear, and she was unaware of the greater reality that was going on – a room full of people at her side. She was safe the entire time, but she had to "see" it for herself before her state changed. My daughter and I couldn't go with Choice #1. We couldn't fall asleep and join her in the illusion to help her fight whatever it was that was showing up in her nightmare. However, we also couldn't wake her up since she had lapsed into a coma. Instead we created Choice #3, a hybrid. We acknowledged what was happening to her while firmly telling her the truth, and while speaking words of comfort, love and compassion.

When our words of truth infiltrated and ultimately penetrated the illusion, she was freed from it.

Hopefully we don't describe our lives as horrific nightmares, but the truth is that when we are living unconsciously, we can get stuck in a dream world of fear and anxiety. Or resentment. Or shame. Or unworthiness. Or inadequacy. These states are as unreal as a dream, and there is always a deeper reality of wholeness available to us – but it is hidden from our awareness. It is there nonetheless.

Words of truth, comfort, love and compassion are continually being whispered to each and every one of us from that deep place of wholeness, courtesy of the Authentic Self. The problem is that the raucous clamoring of the thoughts we habitually entertain easily drowns them out. However, underneath all of the fanfare, there is peace. The same peace that my mother finally sank into is available for anyone who sees through the dream and awakens from unconscious living.

Our red pill can help us find that peace. However, the first hurdle we need to overcome is the fact that just like my mother, we often don't even know we are asleep.

Red Pill Practice

1. What is one situation from your past that you have
   used a translational approach to deal with? It could
   be a job loss, an illness, a relationship issue, etc.

2. Describe the situation and the translational practice
   you used to ease the discomfort.

3. Can you come up with a transformational practice
   that could be used for it?

Chapter 4 Cuz Wakin' Up is Hard to Do

"When one realizes one is asleep, at that moment one is already half-awake." P.D. Ouspensky

It's hard to wake up when you don't realize that you are sleeping.

Unless you are listening to this as an audio book in order to lull yourself to sleep, you are most likely in waking consciousness right now. You are probably aware of the page in front of you and the words you are reading. You may be thinking about the meaning behind them. Take a moment to look around and see what else is in your awareness. Notice that you are not comatose. It *feels* as if you are awake.

And yet, what else may be going on under the surface? There is much that is unseen, traveling under the radar, and things are not always as they seem on the surface. Things are happening all around us that we, as a human species, may not be conscious of at all. Ultraviolet light waves, dog whistles, radio waves, the electromagnetic field of the heart – none of them detectable by the human senses, and yet very much in existence. Although we may not have the receptors to perceive them, these occurrences are as measurable and real as the material and sensory objects that we can touch and feel.

What else might be happening behind the scenes that we don't see or hear, but that are as real as the book or tablet you are holding in your hands right now?

Quantum science tells us that we are 99.999+% empty space, and that what appears solid is really emptiness. So why is it that if I am 99+% empty space and a wall is 99+% empty space, that when we collide it generally goes badly for me? Shouldn't I just pass through like smoke through a screen window? That doesn't seem to be the case, so why is that? What I term "nothing" then is probably something that I can't see.

Research sheds a little more light on this by explaining that there is a force generated through the .001% of "something," and so the wall and I are actually meeting force to force. If that is true, then what is being produced is the real something, and what I view as substance, for instance the physical body, is really a conduit of that force. Quantum researcher Michael Faraday likens it to a fountain spouting water. It is the water that is the force, not the spigot.

What I have been looking at and perceiving to be real, solid, hard, immovable limitation is empty space. And what I have been unable to perceive is, in fact, the real driving force behind the visible world.

Quantum researcher, Dr. Joe Dispenza, tells us that there are 400 billion bits of information available to us in any given moment. And yet we are only making use of 2,000 bits right now.[i] The 2000 bits we pay attention to generally live in the realm of environment, time and the body. Try to picture the massive difference between 400 billion and 2,000 (200 million times). I think you would agree that this is an incredibly significant gap.

Are you up for joining me in a short scientific experiment right now? You won't even need a lab coat. To participate, you will need to stand up and look down at your foot. Now, while you watch it, lightly tap it on the floor. Does the visual perception of your foot touching the floor match the sensation of your foot making contact with it? In other words, can you see and feel your foot hitting the floor at the same moment?

If so, congratulations! You have just done the impossible today.

Why? Because the speed of light is massively faster than the synaptic conduction times needed to get the message from the foot to the brain. So you should *see* it happen *before you feel it* and the lag time should be noticeable. There is actually a Google-worthy name for this phenomenon: *delay and antedating hypothesis paradox.*

There are several thought-provoking theories about why this is so, but the explanation I find most intriguing, and that makes the most sense to me from what I know about brain research, is that both events happen at different times but are experienced together. In other words, the *brain is editing our experience all the time.* And, here's the real kicker. It doesn't *tell us it is doing it*!

We are actually hardwired to be this way since the brain is a sensory organ, designed to interpret and classify our experience on the physical plane for us. If all 400 billion bits were suddenly available to us, what would that be like? The worst acid trip ever. To paraphrase Emily Dickinson, the Truth must dazzle gradually or every person could go blind.

So we need some kind of governing dynamic to help us manage the experience of living in the physical realm. That's all well and good – but the problem for us begins when we forget that we are experiencing life solely through the sensory world, and we think that this is all there is.

What else may be going on that we are unaware of?

Awakening is really about increasing our awareness of the "what else," instead of just buying into what we sense on the surface and thinking that is complete reality. The spiritual teacher Gurdjieff said, "To escape from prison you must first acknowledge that you are in prison, otherwise escape is impossible." The release begins with an acknowledgment that we are often caught in unconscious blue pill living.

The alternative is to remain in slumber and let the few pieces of data, the 2000 bits, that we *do* pay attention to become our total reality as we fill in the blanks with our thoughts, judgments and beliefs. And the icing on the cake is that we happen to have a bias toward noticing the negative things in life.

Red Pill Practice

1. Spend time immersed in nature.

2. Listen deeply and notice the sounds.

3. Focus on deep listening.

4. Try to find the silence that is behind the sound.

Chapter 5 Negativity Bias

"If you are pained by external things, it is not they that disturb you, but your own judgment of them. And it is in your power to wipe out that judgment now." Marcus Aurelius

As a species, we are actually designed to notice and focus on the negative, rather than the positive, as a survival mechanism. Rick Hansen, author of the book *The Buddha's Brain* uses the analogy of Velcro and Teflon to explain how this works. Positive things in our field of awareness tend to slide off us like Teflon, and we take them for granted – while focusing on and sticking to the negative like Velcro, as if our life depended upon it.

Because, in fact, it does.

Let's pretend that you are walking through a forest. It is a bright, sunny day and you are enjoying the smells and sights around you. You have your spouse's boss coming to dinner tomorrow and you are thinking about what you are going to serve, and making a mental list of the ingredients you need to stop and pick up from the grocery store. As you amble along, enjoying the pleasantness of the walk, just cresting the hill on the distant horizon you suddenly spy a huge, black bear heading in your direction.

Thank you, negativity bias. It has just shown you in an instant that if you continue going in the direction you are headed, you will eventually come face to face with the bear. In a split second you make a change in course, and head in the other direction to safety.

It is more important for your survival to see the giant bear lumbering in your direction than it is to notice the beauty of the forest you are now wildly racing through. The bear presents the more pressing problem, and so it is our natural inclination to notice it first. We need this survival mechanism.

After we notice the bear, then what happens internally that helps us to make that beeline in the opposite direction? It is another part of our survival tool kit. An entire system has kicked in that is now helping with the escape. The two main responses that the body is set up to help deal with these kinds of moments are fight and flight. Freeze is actually a higher state of arousal, and it is only a last resort when the other two have been thwarted.

As soon as the negativity bias draws our attention to the danger showing up in our path, the amygdala in the brain immediately springs into action. Known as the "smoke alarm" in the limbic system, it receives the input – a bear approaching – and compares it to memories to determine its safety. What does this remind me of? Do I need to be on guard? Has this happened before?

The limbic system of the brain is very forthcoming with its warnings whenever anything shows up that reminds us of something from the past that may have been dangerous or unsafe. I picture the amygdala as the hapless robot in the '60s sci-fi television program, *Lost in Space,* with arms wildly waving around while shouting "Danger, danger!" at the sign of any hint of possible trouble.

If this wonderful safety mechanism in our brain is showing us that the bear nearby is a danger, we need that information to get away. However, it's important to note that the amygdala can be a bit of an overachiever, and what's worse, it values speed over accuracy. It would rather be wrong 99 times than miss the one time it needed to warn us of danger.

So the bear comes into view off in the distance, the smoke alarm goes off and now the body is flooded with adrenaline and cortisol. The heart rate skyrockets and breathing speeds up. Meanwhile, digestion and cell repair have ceased. That all needs to take a back seat while the blood is busily being directed to the major muscle groups to equip you for your great escape.

Remember the grocery list you were mentally compiling? It is no longer available to you. The higher thinking skills of the brain involved in planning and organizing have gone offline. No time to plan a dinner when you are frantically trying to avoid becoming one.

Hurray for the negativity bias, the amygdala and the fight-or-flight system in the body when a bear is approaching. Together, they have just saved you from becoming the bear's main course.[1]

However, they are not always so helpful.

We don't just activate the survival tool kit when we are in physical danger. The problem arises when it gets triggered by a bear in the form of, say… your ex-boyfriend. Or one of your in-laws. Or your spouse's boss who is coming for dinner. You get the picture.

Things magnify when the negativity bias and the amygdala join together in cahoots.

Fast forward to the next day during dinner. Your nervous system has calmed down and you have worked hard most of the day preparing a wonderful meal. Things seem to be going well. But wait! The negativity bias draws your attention to the fact that your dinner guest seems to be eating very little of the meal, and in fact, is completely avoiding any of the main dish. Now the amygdala eagerly

---

[1] Running from a bear is a really bad idea. So is climbing a tree. They can run and climb very fast. Our hypothetical bear, conjured up for illustration purposes only, is far off in the distance, hasn't spotted you and as luck would have it is upwind. By the way – if you should ever find yourself face to face with a bear, let it see you, look over its shoulder rather than making eye contact, then back or sidle away slowly. And say a prayer or two.

begins comparing notes with past dinner failures and sounds the alarm. Danger, danger!

Adrenaline and cortisol start pumping through your body, and as much as you want to jump up and bolt out of the room in tears, you can't fight or flee, so you freeze, consumed by your inner drama. To top it off, the rational thinking mind goes offline so that you are now unable to put a coherent sentence together. You suffer through the meal, steeped in stress-hormone-enhanced embarrassment and shame-on-steroids. You can add heartburn to the mix, since your digestive system has also shut down.

Later you find out that the boss suffers from severe, life threatening food allergies to the main ingredient in the meal you prepared, and he neglected to tell your spouse. Suddenly all of your angst turns to immense gratitude that he avoided eating it!

The amygdala, in its great rush to serve, actually served up a false alarm. All the drama and suffering was unnecessary. Imagine having the same level of stress from having a meal passed over as seeing a dangerous animal in your path. Consider the wear and tear on the body as the stress response becomes maladaptive.

The problem is that these types of triggering moments are not uncommon, isolated incidents. Most of us can think of multiple times in our lives when we have had those kinds of experiences. School memories, embarrassing moments, adolescence, being shamed, teen years – painful memories may abound! They are ripe for a great deal of potentially dysfunctional "smoke alarm activation."

The stress-response system can be triggered as the amygdala begins warning us of something that is reminiscent of a past hurt, something perceived as dangerous due to a memory from the past. For instance, in school, we may have answered a question incorrectly and been laughed at by others in the class. Because of that experience, if we find ourselves in a similar situation again, the amygdala will sound the alarm and we may experience an internal warning: "Danger, Danger! Do not answer that question! Remember what happened last time when everyone laughed at you. You will make a total fool of yourself again."

For someone being haunted with such a painful memory, this kind of experience can be as scary as a bear approaching. Now fast forward a few decades and that same dynamic can still be showing up, thanks to our internal cranial smoke alarm. And maybe the behavior that is exhibited as an adult is that in a group setting, you have the tendency to be very cautious about speaking your mind, because the amygdala is giving the same warning.

The stress-response system is not designed for long-term, chronic overuse. It is intended specifically for acute threats and problems. Having this system triggered over and over is like calling 911 every week because your teenage son is running late picking you up with your car. Although we might all agree that that is high on the annoyance scale, the system is not designed to deal with such things, and it would get overtaxed trying to manage issues like these.

What happens if this sound-the-alarm way of relating to what is showing up in our life becomes the norm for us? Repeated triggering of the stress-response system creates neural architecture in the brain that becomes our hard-wiring, courtesy of a phenomenon known as *synaptic potentiation*.

Firing and Wiring Together

The brain is made up of billions of nerve cells called neurons. As we learn and experience new things, the neurons are all busily connecting with one another as they fire electrochemical information back and forth. If we keep thinking the same thoughts and repeating the same experiences, the neurons continue to fire in the same way, creating a stronger connection. After a while, this neural pathway becomes a well-traveled route.

This is very helpful if we are learning to play the piano, for instance. At first when we sit down to play, it feels awkward and difficult. The more repetitive practice we engage in, the neurons that are firing together over and over begin to wire together. Suddenly our fingers are flying over those piano keys, and it is feeling more and more natural because of our well-worn *Habit Highway*.

But what if the habit we are creating is to chronically trigger the stress response? The same synaptic potentiation happens. Our neural connections support and strengthen the habitual response as it becomes the easiest pathway to follow and turns into our default route. It's like getting stuck in a rut. Habit is simply a repetitive neurological loop. When these default patterns are running us, we get stuck on high alert.

The effects of constantly overtaxing the stress-response system are significant. In fact, according to the authors of *The Healing Code,*[ii] stress is the culprit behind fully 90% of our illnesses. Scientific study reported by the Institute of HeartMath confirms that the chronic release of stress hormones is a major contributing factor for numerous health issues. The list is extensive, and it includes: accelerated aging, brain-cell death, decreased muscle mass and bone density, impaired memory and learning, weakened immune system, reduced skin growth and regeneration, increased blood sugar and fat accumulation.[iii]

Wait, fat accumulation? Stress does *that*? Yes, it even does *that*.

So the negativity bias, while very handy in life-or-death situations, actually diminishes in usefulness when it becomes our habitual way of looking at life. We can get stuck in a loop of seeing what's wrong in our world and actually become addicted to an inner experience of negativity!

Red Pill Practice

1. Take a moment and sit in a comfortable position.

2. Move your attention to your feet and feel them on the floor.

3. Slowly let your focus widen as you become aware of your legs, the trunk of your body, your shoulders, arms and hands.

4. Feel your neck, scalp and face.

5. Really inhabit your body.

6. Now feel the sensations, emotions and feelings throughout your body.

7. Observe what is going on that may have previously escaped your notice.

8. Experience your aliveness.

Chapter 6 Addicted to Negativity

"What is addiction, really? It is a sign, a signal, a symptom of distress. It is a language that tells us about a plight that must be understood." – Alice Miller

Addictions come in many guises. With some, it is the more obviously self-destructive ones to drugs, alcohol, or dangerous eating disorders. With others, it can be subtler forms of addictive behavior – excessive exercise, work, shopping, video games, use of social media, for example. These can easily fly under the radar of social acceptance. But their origins remain the same – a desire to escape the present moment, and to cover up the unconscious depleting emotional ocean that lies buried inside.

But what do you do when you are actually *addicted* to the negativity of that emotional ocean? Dr. Dispenza tells us that there are different chemicals activated for every emotional state that we experience in our day-to-day lives, and when these states become chronic, it can actually cause a biochemical addiction. The more often we feel the emotion, the more addicted we become. As the body's cells divide, the new ones need more of those chemicals to get the same stimulation as the old cell.

When we chronically feel stressed out, anxious, depressed or bored, this becomes our habituated state of being. Then when we are *not* feeling that way, something doesn't seem quite right and we develop behaviors that can help us get our fix! It's called self-sabotage and if left unchecked, it can undermine our well-being.

So not only am I prone to notice and focus on the negative in order to survive and be safe, I can actually have an addiction to feeling down and depressed. These negative emotional states can overwhelm, and in a sense, even steal our lives from us.

What a setup.

Think of all of the ways that emotional addiction affects life as we know it – how seductively unifying it can be to join in with others awash in righteous anger, how misery loves company, what it feels like to be an "adrenaline junkie" or being trapped in chronic anxiety. To be caught in an addictive cycle and driven by the need for a bio-chemical rush is the epitome of unconscious behavior.

Being hard-wired to look for what might be a danger or a threat predisposes us to pay attention to and focus on what's not working. This pre-programmed automatic negativity comes so naturally to us that we don't even realize we are doing it.

I awakened to this discovery one day as I was attempting to lift myself out of a mildly depressed state and get excited about an upcoming vacation. Somehow, this was surprisingly difficult to do. I found myself being quite comfortable wallowing in the ruts of pessimism and hopelessness, and it seemed as though trying to climb out of it was as daunting as scaling a rock wall without a harness. Why was I having such a difficult time getting there? I finally realized that this depressed state was a habit that had actually become an addiction, and I needed to make a change that would lift me out of that addictive trance.

And the good news is that things *can* change!

Pavlov's famous dogs were conditioned to salivate at the sounding of a bell that was associated with receiving food. However, after the bell rang repeatedly *without* food, the dogs *stopped* salivating at the sound. Their conditioned behavior changed with a different stimulus. In the same way, our conditioned patterns of behavior can also change as we do something new.

In order to shift this behavior of focusing on the negative, it takes an intentional practice that helps to counterbalance this tendency and begin to re-route the mental architecture that has supported this habitual way of behaving. In order to forge a new path, we have to make a different choice – and continue making that choice – until it becomes the new habit. For me to awaken from this kind of addictive sleepwalking through life, I have to stop myself in a triggering moment, take time to pause, realize that the brain's negativity bias has kicked in and then consciously take a new route.

I have to shift my perception from noticing what is wrong to actively looking for what is right. Which lens we look through to view our life matters a great deal – since experiences themselves are actually neutral, and it is actually our internal reaction to them that determines the stress level they cause us.

What we see is mitigated by how we perceive the world, and we are stuck in misperception more often than we might realize.

Perception Correction

"It ain't what you don't know that gets you into trouble. It's what you know for sure that just ain't so." Mark Twain

My brother burst into the room where I was sitting, and clearly agitated, blurted out, "I'm tired of all the sex around here!"

His statement was odd for a number of reasons, although two topped the list.

First, there was the fact that he was six years old and had no conception of what "all the sex around here" would even mean. I, as his older sister, barely had an inkling.

Second, and frankly, the more alarming of the two to my adolescent mind, was that the only other people who were at home at the time were our parents and our visiting grandmother. If he was witnessing a lot of sex going on, something was *beyond* very wrong. My stomach threatened to heave at the very thought.

As my face took on a look of horror and my mouth curled into a Jimmy Fallon-esque "ewwww," he added, "Every time I ask Mom for something, all she ever says is "Wait a sec. Wait a sec. Wait a sec." And he stomped out of the room in disgust.

He wasn't tired of all the sex; he was tired of all the secs.

The retching in my stomach instantly morphed into an uncontrollable belly laugh.

This encounter became a fairly infamous childhood story that was revisited at most every family gathering thereafter, and never failed to provide a highly entertaining source of amusement for us all. Even my brother saw the humor after a while.

I learned something very valuable that day, although I couldn't put it into words until much later in life – but I had participated in a classic case of misperception. Have you ever misunderstood what someone said to you, thinking it meant one thing but discovering it meant quite another?

It happens all the time because our mind judges and makes meaning of what we perceive to be happening around us. In addition, it creates a narrative around our perception – or, as in the case of the incident with my brother, our misperception. My mind was busily making up a story that even had potential physiological effects for me.

Observer Effect

As it turns out, perception has a lot of clout. We can't just observe reality; we interact with it. Just by the act of observing, we alter the object of observation as well as the observer itself.

This discovery comes from an experiment in which researchers were trying to determine if light was a particle or a wave, since it exhibited both dynamics. Interestingly, it was revealed that if there was a measuring device "observing" during the process, its behavior changed. It interacted with the wave and collapsed it into a particle. The scientists concluded that light was both a particle *and* a wave, and that its behavior depended upon the observer.

The wave is a field of infinite possibilities out of which a particle emerges in the context of an observer's perspective. In other words, just by observing, we participate in co-creating the experience.

So the term *observer effect* refers to the alteration that the act of observation will make on the phenomenon that is being observed. We can apply the observer effect metaphorically to our own lives as we consider how we are seeing our world. We alter reality by paying attention to it, and our way of perceiving can change the course of our personal histories.

There is a beautiful line in the book *A Course in Miracles* that never fails to help me shift my perception. It is, "I could see peace instead of this." Observing with the heart, our vision becomes clear. Seeing with the eyes of appreciation, compassion and forgiveness – we change our viewing point and see a different world. Our life shifts and changes depending upon our perspective.

If I look through a window that is covered in mud, the car in the driveway looks like it could use a good scrub down even if I have spent the whole afternoon washing and waxing it. Clean the window, and suddenly the car is sparkling too.

The problem is that we are misperceiving all the time and don't realize it! Due to the prolific quantity of "false positives" that our overachieving amygdala feeds us, the possibility of misperception grows by leaps and bounds. In addition, we are seeing through the complex filtering system comprised of our beliefs, judgments, myths and unconscious thoughts, and not recognizing the deeper reality. With such static to try to peer through, how can we ever hope to see things clearly?

Living beneath the threshold of our perceptions, however, the wise reasoning of the heart can provide a different, more empowering viewpoint. The answer is to look through the portal of the heart. As the Swiss psychiatrist/psychotherapist Carl Jung so beautifully writes, "Your vision will become clear only when you look into your heart. Who looks outside, dreams. Who looks inside, awakens."

The antidote for dealing with misperception is to look inside and call upon the wisdom of the heart to provide a "perception correction" using a red pill practice called appreciation.

And the good news is, it only takes a few secs.

Red Pill Practice

1. Describe a time when you mistakenly had a misperception about a person or a situation that caused some stress or conflict.

2. What did you think was happening?

3. What was actually happening?

4. What effect did your misperception have on the person or situation?

Chapter 7 The Red Pill Antidote: An Attitude of Gratitude

"In the present moment we are always greeted by the fragrance of gratitude." Michael Brown

A large two-engine train was crossing the country. After it had gone some distance, one of the engines broke down.

"No problem," the engineer thought, and carried on at half power. Farther on down the line, the other engine broke down and the train came to a standstill.

The engineer decided he should inform the passengers about why the train had stopped, and made the following announcement, "Ladies and gentlemen, I have some good news and some bad news. The bad news is that both engines have failed and we will be stuck here for some time." He could hear the sound of rising angry voices.

Then he added, "The good news is that you are not in an airplane." The angry voices melted into laughter. It very quickly changed everyone's perception from one of condemnation to one of gratitude.

As the Nazi prison-camp survivor Viktor Frankl insightfully reminds us, there is power in the pause between stimulus and response. To eclipse the effects of the automatic fight/flight stimulus-response mechanism that springs into action during triggering moments, we have a tool to use that provides a powerful pause. We access that tool by activating a feeling of heartfelt appreciation. Gratitude is the magic key to changing our focus and our inner state, and we connect with it through the power of the heart.

By creating a daily habit of looking for what is working and then feeling grateful for it, we begin to shift our perception from watching for what could go wrong, to being on the lookout for the goodness of life and cultivating the powerful "red pill practice" of appreciation.

To be clear, I am not referring to an anemic, wimpy, feeble or passive form of thankfulness here.

I am talking about a dynamic, generative, proactive powerhouse of appreciation – what New Thought minister David Owen Ritz refers to as "kick-your-butt" gratitude. By a daily, hourly and eventually moment-by-moment practice of feeling appreciation, we can generate a positive, harmonious energy field from the heart that can cause our life experience to "appreciate in value."

We get beyond habitual patterns of perception when we shift our focus from what we don't want that has been showing up in our lives, to what is working and what we can be thankful for. And the really cool part is that we will find whatever we are looking for.

I read about a wonderful practice that a young Nepalese girl had taken on that she called having "gratitude achievement" moments. The woman who wrote about this was volunteering in Nepal and when she heard the girl say gratitude *achievement* she thought it was perhaps a mistranslation of English. But no, the girl meant gratitude achievement. I like to term it *anticipatory appreciation.* Instead of or in addition to sitting down at the end of the day and reflecting on things to be grateful for, she looked ahead to her day and chose three moments that she expected to be joyful ones, set the intention to feel gratitude and then she would let it all go. When each of those moments arrived, she would remember that it was a moment that she was waiting to be grateful for.

This is generative, proactive gratitude. Anticipatory appreciation. When I read about it, I decided to give it a try. During a time of early morning stillness, I looked ahead to my day and chose three moments. The first was when I would be enjoying breakfast with my husband, a second one was when I had completed revising some writing I was working on and my third choice was when I planned to call my daughter in the late afternoon. I envisioned each of these experiences, saw my day flowing with ease, and then amped up the gratitude in my heart as I anticipated them. Finally, I let it all go and went on with my day.

So what happened?

I was sitting at breakfast and enjoying the meal when suddenly I felt a surge of gratitude for the healthy food, for the ambience of the room, for the conversation we were having. And I said, "I remember that this is a moment I was waiting to be grateful for!"

Then I started working on the revisions, and as I had earlier foreseen, there was a wonderful flow about it that made it so much easier than it had been in the past. I found myself completing the writing much quicker than expected, and as I stepped away from the computer, I remembered, "This is a moment I was waiting to be grateful for!" And my heart opened in joyful appreciation for the experience of flow, for the guidance I had received in my writing and for the total ease with which the words had emerged.

Hey, this stuff was working!

Later on, I pulled out my phone and as I clicked on my daughter's number, I stopped and remembered, "This is a moment I was waiting to be grateful for!" And again, I was flooded with deep appreciation, and feelings of immense gratitude.

I realized something important. By setting an intention to experience these anticipatory appreciation moments, I was setting into motion a subconscious command to stop, return my awareness to the present moment and feel the gratitude. When you are present, you cannot *help* but feel grateful. As Michael Brown, author of *The Presence Process*, very insightfully reminds us with such poetic beauty, gratitude is the very fragrance of the present moment. In other words, being present to this moment, you automatically feel saturated in deep appreciation.

This doesn't mean that we have to wait for those moments to feel gratitude, or that we can't pause and be grateful for whatever is showing up. It also doesn't mean that we can't have a moment of gratitude at the end of our day when we take stock of all of the blessings. Anticipatory appreciation can be a wonderful addition to any gratitude practice that we already have.

As I worked with it, I discovered the potential it had to awaken me to the magnificence of the present moment. Consequently, I found myself bathed in gratitude throughout my day.

Anticipatory appreciation is an excellent "red pill practice" that can serve as an antidote to the addictive negativity bias. In order to do that, we need to shift our focus and activate our built-in ability to shift attention. We actually do this pivoting practice all the time. For instance, imagine that you decide to buy a new car, and as you search, you become interested in a certain make and model – maybe even a particular color. What happens next? Suddenly now, wherever you go, you see that type of car. They are showing up everywhere.

I call it The Black Dress Syndrome.

One Christmas, my grandmother shared with the family that she had always wanted a fancy black dress. Suddenly my mother and I were on a mission to find her one. I am sure I discovered every single black dress that was hanging in every woman's clothing store within a radius of twenty miles. I would walk through the doors of a shop, and suddenly every black dress in the store would be shouting my name. Everywhere I looked, they seemed to leap off the racks. I could zero in and spot a black dress from a mile away. After weeks of hunting, my mother and I celebrated our success when we finally found the dress that we bought for her, but it took some time before black dresses receded from my attention viewfinder. We have that power to shift our focus, and in so doing, to see things differently. What we focus on, we find.

If I start to focus on what is working in my life, it shifts my outlook to one of "Everything is happening for my good," and I start to look through that lens. The more I look for things to appreciate, the more I find them. The awakened heart means a heart that is alive and communicating with the vibration of gratitude. Gratitude magnifies the blessings in our lives and endows whatever is showing up with the capacity to be a gift. It also changes our physiology to a more harmonious state, and it is the key to unlocking the deeper heart intelligence within.

Neuroscientists have discovered that gratitude activates the parts of the brain that produce dopamine and serotonin – the "feel good" hormones. In addition, the regular practice of searching for something to appreciate actually helps to develop emotional intelligence, which in turn generates more gratitude.

The Institute of HeartMath has done extensive research on the physiological effects of positive emotion. By focusing on the heart and allowing feelings of love and appreciation to expand and radiate outward, we enable our systems to come into alignment. An ordered, coherent state is created in the body, a feeling they describe as "amplified peace."

Remember all the negative effects of stress? Activating positive emotions appears to be an effective antidote. Feelings of appreciation can lower the stress hormone cortisol, and increase production of the revitalizing, so-called anti-aging hormone DHEA, which typically decreases with age.

In a scientific study on the effects of both anger and compassion on the immune system, researchers found that *five minutes* of anger impaired the immune system for up to six hours, while five minutes of feeling a positive emotion such as appreciation *enhanced* the immune system. As Voltaire wisely declared, "I have decided to be happy because it's good for my health."

It appears that feeling good is, in fact, good for you. And just think of it. By practicing this, we can help bring peace to our world *and* lose weight. Truly a win-win!

Appreciation is a simple feeling to generate because typically we can find something or someone to appreciate no matter what is going on. I have had times of great stress and worry, and when I take a gratitude break, I think of my beloved grandchildren. Immediately, my heart opens in appreciation. We can think about people or pets that we love, cherished memories, or a place of beauty. Whatever we choose to use, it needs to produce a *feeling* of appreciation; we don't want to just *think* about it.

Remember, this is kick-your-butt gratitude we are talking about here.

The more we feel appreciation, the more internal harmony we create as all of the body's systems come into alignment, and eventually entrain with the coherent signal that is created. As an added benefit, the effect is cumulative. The more we practice, the more coherence we add to our emotional bank account. Eventually it becomes our baseline response as the neural pathways carve their way into a habitual behavior.

When we catch ourselves looking at life through the lens of the negativity bias, noticing what is wrong, we then shift into the heart and activate appreciation – a new, life-affirming emotion. Suddenly our eyes are opened to whatever mental melodrama we have been entertaining, and we can self-distance enough to see it objectively. Rather than being mired in negativity and having it be our only option, appreciation allows us to step out of that well-traveled rut, and choose to give our attention to the blessings that have always been present.

It may be true that as human beings we have a negativity bias, but awakening to that pattern of behavior and being aware of when it is being activated puts the power of the moment back into our hands. Understanding that there is an actual addiction to feeling the emotions that we typically feel gives us the insight and inspiration to begin replacing chronic depression or anger by consciously activating feelings of appreciation. This can lead to peace, love and joy. It takes some work to create new neural pathways for that to become habitual, but the truth is, we each have the ability to be the vehicle for these higher attributes of the Authentic Self within us.

Melody Beattie writes, "Gratitude unlocks the fullness of life. It turns what we have into enough, and more. It turns denial into acceptance, chaos to order, confusion to clarity. It can turn a meal into a feast, a house into a home, a stranger into a friend. Gratitude makes sense of our past, brings peace for today, and creates a vision for tomorrow."

That about says it.

Red Pill Practice

This is a powerful process that can bring peace, harmony and coherence to your mind, body and emotions in a few minutes of practice.

1. Make a list of people and/or things that can bring forth a feeling of appreciation for you. They can be people, pets, cherished memories and/or beautiful

scenes in nature. You don't just want to think about it, you want to *feel* it.

2. Stop, breathe, feel. Where are you right now? Feel your feet, your legs, the trunk of your body. Feel your shoulders, arms, hands, neck, head. Are you all in? Feel your aliveness.

3. Let appreciation pour forth from your heart as you bring into your mind's eye someone or something that you deeply appreciate from your list.

4. Let the appreciation rise up, expand and radiate from your heart through your body.

5. Let it fill your body. Imagine every cell bathed in this glorious vibration.

6. Feel it move beyond the body. Let it fill the room, and then send it, beam it, radiate it outward.

Chapter 8 Orphaned

"The most exhausting thing in my life is being insincere."
Anne Morrow Lindbergh

I joined a club one day that I didn't even know existed, and frankly never had any desire to be a part of. It's called "Adults Whose Parents Have Died." As you approach your later wisdom years, the membership grows significantly in this club, although it is not exclusive of any age. At the age of 69, my beloved mother was diagnosed with inflammatory breast cancer, one of the most aggressive and painful forms, and struggled for four years to heal from it.

Her doctor had told her when he gave her the diagnosis that she had about four months to live and that it wouldn't be pretty. This type of cancer spreads like wildfire and in its final stages can eventually end up on the outside of the body, with open sores that never heal. Of course, she didn't tell any of us this news. She kept it firmly inside and declared that she was confident she would beat it. In fact, she was *determined* to and this became her theme song, "I'm not going anywhere!" She repeated that mantra endlessly, all the way to her deathbed, four years later.

She struggled for those four years, trying various herbal remedies, chemotherapy, radiation, surgery, fasting, juicing – all to no avail. The disease marched on and spread from one breast to the other, to the spine, to the hip, to the neck. And then... sores on the stomach, spreading to the back and arms.

I am not sure what is more painful, the prospect of having your mother gone from this physical realm or watching her suffer month by month and painfully disintegrate before your eyes. When she died, although I grieved deeply for the loss, I also felt immense relief that her intense suffering was now over.

After my mom's funeral, I spoke to a woman I had recently met. "I am so sorry to hear about your mother," she said. "Mine died twelve years ago, and there isn't a day that goes by that I don't think of her." She understood.

Then she asked if my father was still alive. Yes, he was – drowning in grief, but still very much alive. "Ah," she answered, "then you aren't an orphan yet." Her words took my breath away and I actually gasped in surprise. Orphan! The word left me cold. I walked away from that conversation feeling shaken, with visions of Oliver Twist and his empty bowl in my hands.

Who knew that only a few weeks later, the unthinkable would actually happen? My father, after having dinner with my brother and two aunts, sat in his favorite easy chair and dozed off. Landing with a thud on the floor, he was instantly dead of a massive heart attack.

Stunned and deeply shaken, I found myself at a second funeral very much like the first – same church, same people, much more of a shock. With no desire on my part, my membership in the club had been expanded.

I had indeed become an orphan.

I was unprepared for the psycho-spiritual shock that was unleashed. Despite having a very supportive spouse and loving children of my own, with both parents so suddenly gone, I found myself wandering in the wilderness for a while in a state of orphaned isolation – feeling lost, alone, and on my own. Who would comfort me now or have my back? Where was the nurturing parental caring and compassion that I had always enjoyed and now so desperately needed? My two biggest cheerleaders and comforters had left the planet.

Slowly it dawned on me that I had "moved up the food chain" so to speak. Now *I* was the elder in my family, and instead of looking outside of myself to find peace and comfort, it was up to me to find it within myself and then to not only nurture myself but to pass it along down the line.

As I walked through this experience of feeling so bereft of love and caring, it struck me that these feelings of being abandoned were all too familiar to me. As I delved deeper, I discovered that they were linked to having my own *internal* orphans. The death of both of my parents in such a short amount of time shone a light on what had been in there all along. In essence, within our psyche, we all have little Dickens characters roaming around – in the guise of disowned and disconnected parts of ourselves – which we have abandoned. Orphans.

Carl Jung gives us insight as to how these orphaned parts are created. We are born knowing only oneness, undifferentiated, believing that, "Everything is me." At this early stage, there is no distinction occurring as of yet between self and other, and therefore no sense of "self" exists. Everything is subjective in this state, and it is not until we move into toddlerhood in the early pre-conventional childhood years that we begin to differentiate, understanding that there is "me" and "other," and developing a sense of separate selfhood. This becomes the formation of the ego.

As we trace the developmental process from infant to young adult, we witness the slow but steady acclimation into cultural socialization. We learn how to function in the physical realm, learning little by little how to make sense and meaning of it. The formation of a healthy ego is actually part of a developmental, progressive, age-related process.

During these formative years, we come into this world needing two things, love and protection. Depending on how well those needs are met in our early years, we will make decisions about ourselves and about the world. Often, what rises up is a negative opinion of our own value and worth. Throughout that time, at some precognitive level, we all experienced moments when we didn't get the love and protection we needed to manage developmental stresses. Perhaps we got yelled at and pulled back from crossing the road in a manner that made us think we were bad. Perhaps our parents weren't there for us in some way when we needed them. It could have been that at that moment dinner was burning and they needed to drop everything and deal with it.

Without the mental capability to view ourselves and our experience in a reflective context, we personalized the pain of not having our needs met. Over countless vulnerable and impressionable moments like these, because our needs were not met in some fashion, and depending upon our level of cognitive development, we may have reached incorrect, faulty conclusions about ourselves, our family, our friends and the world, which eventually grew into beliefs.

Limiting beliefs such as "I am not good enough"; "I am not lovable"; The world is not safe"; "There is something wrong with me"; "I am not valuable"; "I don't matter"; "People can't be trusted" and so on, are often birthed from this period of our lives and can become the filter through which we view the world. They cause us to interpret life through a haze of false perceptions. These beliefs were taken on before we had the cognitive capacity for abstract thinking, sometimes even in preverbal stages of childhood.

On top of that, from the ages of two until about six, a child is in the Theta range of brain-wave patterns. In this slower frequency, which is the realm of imagination, critical thinking has not yet emerged. For this reason, children at this stage are very likely to believe what they are told – and whatever it is, it tends to go directly into the subconscious mind. The memories are recorded at the reasoning level we had attained at the time. At Theta, experiences are directly hard-wired into the subconscious without the benefit of being filtered through any measure of mature discernment.

Do you see a potential problem with any of this?

It adds up like so:

> Not always getting needs met around love and protection
> + hearing less-than-loving words
> + having immature cognitive development
> + Theta brain waves
> = taking on limiting beliefs

Are you with me so far?

We tried to repress or disown these parts of our psyche that we thought to be unlovable, not good enough or not measuring up, since they were too painful to look at full on. We sent them underground but they didn't go away. They became buried in our subconscious, and although we may not even be aware of them, the truth is that they unconsciously affect our lives. Jung refers to them as "hungry dogs in the basement." Avoiding them, ignoring these aspects of the unconscious, pretending they don't exist or denying their presence will not heal them. They just get hungrier and noisier.

As the daughter of poet Audre Lorde describes it, "There's always that one little piece inside you that wants to be spoken out, and if you keep ignoring it, it gets madder and madder and hotter and hotter, and if you don't speak out one day it will just up and punch you in the mouth from the inside."

Hate it when *that* happens. With the death of both of my parents, I was definitely being punched in the mouth from the inside.

These unintegrated aspects of our psyche become the shadow, wreaking havoc in our lives as unconscious patterns that dictate our behavior. As Jung describes it, it is like burying dynamite. The orphaned parts create a divided life, forming an "inner fault line" between what we believe to be acceptable and not acceptable. This internal divide is then transmitted into our world and mirrored back to us in some way.

We learn very early on to mask what we believe to be the unacceptable parts, and then we hide behind the mask. In an effort to uphold a false image we have, we learn short-term, self-protective solutions that try to mask the pain – resistance, defensiveness, avoidance. Eventually they become our typical "blue pill" behavioral responses. We will be drawn to people and situations that reflect and reinforce the persona, our acceptable side, and will want to push away or run from people who remind us of the shadow, which mirrors the unacceptable side.

At the same time, we can project the shadow onto others, finding something wrong with *them*. It's a lot easier to project the painful thought I have about myself, and focus on another person's behavior, than it is to admit that I share that behavior. This unconscious behavior pattern becomes part of our default operating system and we start living a myth that we have accepted as truth in our lives.

The persona, or acceptable side, is the self we consciously believe ourselves to be. It is the face we show to the world and it becomes the foundation of a false identity, the ego.

Red Pill Practice

1. Describe a time when you used resistance, avoidance or needing to be right as a defensive coping strategy.

2. What was the result of using that strategy?

Chapter 9 Bloated Nothingness

"Let us take our bloated nothingness out of the path of the divine circuits." Ralph Waldo Emerson

One of the definitions of the word, EGO using the letters of the word, is: *Edging God Out* – although a more accurate, yet slightly less acronym-friendly description might be *Eclipsing Our Awareness of Authentic Wholeness.* It refers to the egoic overshadowing of the experience of our indwelling wholeness. Awakening leads us to discovering that wholeness through the realization that the self I have taken to be the totality of who I am is *not* the complete picture. We pull back the curtain – and we see that the wizard is *not* the great and powerful Oz.

There is nothing inherently bad or wrong with the ego; it's just that it isn't the whole enchilada. The ego lives in a world that does not acknowledge any other dimensions of living. It's like an actor or actress believing that the role being played is the entirety of who he or she is, and completely forgetting that the greater part exists behind the mask. Although the ego may be a useful component of the navigation system needed in our journey through sensory world, we have, in effect, allowed it to be in the captain's chair when it doesn't belong there. It has been given a job that it was never designed to do. It isn't equipped to be Captain Kirk – aside perhaps from its flair for the overly dramatic – but it could be a very useful and valuable First Officer Spock.

The identity that we have bought into has been created through years of life experiences and decades of social programming, and it is undergirded with the collective trance of cultural indoctrination. We are, as physicist Sean Carroll describes it, "bubbling cauldrons of preferences, wants, sentiments, aspirations, likes, feelings, attitudes, predilections, values, and devotions."

To help us see how attached we are to the ego as an identity, there is a mental exercise we can try: For one whole day, go without using the word "I." On second thought, forget the whole day. Try it for an hour. It is challenging, to say the least. You find yourself saying alien sentences as, "There is an experience of love rising up." "There is anger brewing from within because the dishes aren't done." We discover just how much our world and our communication revolve around the "I."

And yet this "I," the normal waking consciousness that we have bought into believing to be who we are, is really nothing more than a set of thoughts, beliefs and stories that we have taken on – many of them disempowering ones. This self becomes a "structure of knowing" in which we live. We can think of it as a dwelling place of safety for the ego, complete with protective walls, lockable doors, skeletons in the closet, scary basements, dust-laden attics and windows badly in need of cleaning. We peer through these partially shuttered windowpanes, obscured by beliefs, myths and judgments, as we perceive a world based on what we look through. Essentially all egoic perception is really misperception because it is incomplete, personal, and driven by beliefs, values and emotions. Not to mention, it is projected!

Eckhart Tolle once said, "When you realize that there is a voice in your head that pretends to be you and never stops speaking, you are awakening out of your unconscious identification with the stream of thinking. Knowing yourself as the awareness behind the voice is freedom."

That freedom is not available to us if we are looking through a lens that is unconsciously dictated by our past history, which stems from faulty beliefs that we took on before we were developmentally able to see that they weren't true! No wonder the world is awash in a sea of conflict, misunderstanding and confusion.

This incomplete and non-existent egoic identity, "bloated nothingness" as Emerson describes it, is the personality that we have believed ourselves to be. While being completely ill equipped to captain a ship, it has nevertheless been attempting to do so. We have largely been unconscious of this fact – unaware that the real captain has been usurped.

So who does belong in the captain's chair? Our Authentic Self. And the good news is that it has never vacated the seat. It is just waiting quietly and patiently for us to notice.

The I's Have It

"When we shift out of ego-identification, we can recognize our own thoughts, feelings and subpersonalities as changing contents of consciousness." Loch Kelly

Transcending the ego is not about killing off part of ourselves or getting rid of it. Rather, it is about recognizing the ego as the limited self that we want to bring into maturity. As Richard Rohr celebrates, "The final, stupendous gift is that your false self becomes the raw material for your unique version of True Self." Transcending the limited self, we then gently, and with compassion, take it out of the driver's seat, becoming free of its grip and letting the greater Authentic Self take over. The first thing you discover is the relief that comes from relinquishing the role of impersonating the captain and letting Spirit lead. It is exhausting trying to be who we are not.

With our Authentic Self as the coach, the ego becomes a valued team member. We need a healthy, mature ego to help navigate the physical, embodied realm. When there is a beneficial relationship and healthy interplay between the Authentic Self and the ego, this is a sign of developing spiritual intelligence.

How do we know when we are stuck in ego? Well, if our thinking is limited, controlling, defending, being right, chances are good that it is ego-driven behavior. The ego loves, loves, loves to look good and be glorified. Conversely, it is a shattering experience for the ego to look bad. It lives in fear of being exposed in any way. Thinking only inside the box, feeling like a fraud, clinging to what is safe, afraid of stepping outside the comfort zone of our structure of knowing, and overly conditioned by fear of being laughed at or of being wrong – all of these are learned behaviors that result from letting this bloated nothingness be in charge. So, if we find ourselves being triggered in some way, by people and situations around us, we need to pay attention to that. Close attention. It's a clue that the ego is on the scene.

From Ego to We-Grow

"You must unlearn what you have learned." Yoda

The spiritual teacher Adyashanti writes, "What we call ego is simply the mechanism our mind uses to resist life as it is." By being against something, the ego is actually strengthened. Since these resistant egoic patterns have been learned, that means they can also be unlearned. As the Jedi master Yoda tells us, it's about unlearning what we have learned.

Rather than banishing parts of ourselves to languish in a netherworld, we want to use this unlearning as the avenue to reintegrate the orphaned parts that we have believed to be unlovable. We are then free to welcome them back into our psyche so that we can stop being run by them! It's not about getting rid of the ego, it is about finding an antidote to its "chain-reactivity." Integration disarms the internal resistor and as we strip away all this stuff, what do we find? As the great unlearning takes place, blockages are removed and what is revealed is our Authentic Self, the Jedi that already lives within us!

Until we do this work, however, the orphaned parts will continue to cleverly hide in the recesses of the psyche and keep on messing up – like unruly children trying to make their presence known.

Stephen Glenn and Jane Nelson report on research that shows that children who are confident in their capability, who believe in their personal significance and their capacity to make a difference, tend to grow and develop their potential. On the other hand, they write that "young people who believe they are incapable and insignificant and that whatever happens is beyond their control tend to live life by default and reaction." It is important to change those accumulated, deeply encoded, mistaken beliefs no matter what chronological age we are now.

It is tempting to cast the blame for our dilemma on those adults or peers who were a part of our early life. However, this is not about blaming our parents, teachers or the classroom bully for the disowning of our Authentic Self and creation of the shadow. It really is a part of being born into the human condition. As Samuel Beckett puts it, "You're on planet Earth. There is no cure for that."

It is a consequence of the human condition that comes from growing up in an imperfect caregiving environment and a culture that reinforces egoic behavior. Each of our parents was born into it, and their parents, and theirs, on up the line. We all participate in this! If the unconscious default operating system continues unchecked, then we, in turn, pass it on to our children. It is our shared humanity.[2]

What has happened is not our *fault*. But we *can* take responsibility for no longer being at the mercy of the faulty decisions we made before having the cognitive ability to reason otherwise. If we don't take responsibility, these orphaned parts of ourselves will just continue to run our lives without our awareness. Like a dwelling place with an absentee landlord, things will continue to run amuck.

Awakening means becoming aware of when these old, limiting egoic patterns are running the show. Then, instead of letting them automatically dictate our behavior, we take steps to change and transform. We need a practice that helps us gain self-awareness of the blue pill behavior that is within us, and then integrate whatever is in the way of our experience of Reality.

---

[2] *To be clear – this doesn't mean we condone or downplay the possible traumatic effect of childhood abuse. It can have severe consequences in the damaging of a child's psyche, and a deeper therapeutic approach to healing may be what is required. If you have suffered from childhood abuse, we suggest finding a therapist that you trust and letting him or her accompany and guide you on your healing journey.*

It is the alignment between mind and heart that does the healing work. This wholeheartedness overrides the ego – and the ego returns to its true purpose, of serving the Authentic Self and helping with the navigation, instead of insisting on taking the wheel.

Live long and prosper.

If I'm Not Me, Then Who Am I?

"I didn't realize who I was until I stopped being who I wasn't." Sri Gawn Tu Fahr, aka Jean-Pierre Gregoire

So, if I am not the ego-self that I have thought myself to be, then who am I? While we may have identified with many labels throughout our lives – brother, sister, spouse, child, parent, teacher, friend – the labels simply describe relationships that we have had and roles that we have occupied.

Who are we without our labels?

We begin to catch a glimpse of a deeper dimension of Reality underneath it all when we take the red pill. We might call it Higher Power, Divine Essence, Noble Heart, Greater Mind, Pure Awareness, the Christ, Buddha Nature, Indwelling Spirit, Soul, Sacred Self, the One, Atman, Presence. My preferred term is the Authentic Self. Whatever name we use, it refers to our shared inherent spiritual potential, the Divine treasure sheltered within every heart, the very aliveness of Spirit that animates all beings. We are each individualized expressions of the One Life, repositories of the Infinite.

The Sufi creation story tells it beautifully like this: In the beginning of Time, the Creator wanted to behold the beauty of Creation, and so a mirror was fashioned. As the mirror was held up to the Creator's face, says the legend, so great was the light and the power and the beauty of the image that the mirror shattered into billions of bright, shiny pieces of every size and shape and color and description. Thus were the people of the world created: reflections of Spirit and all unique facets of the One.

We are reflections of One Spirit, all wearing various costumes. As Ernest Holmes put it, "Your mind is an outlet through which the Creative Intelligence of the universe seeks fulfillment."

The point is that we are w-a-a-a-y more than we appear to be!

As we connect with the Authentic Self, we have access to the wisdom and guidance of the heart. When we dig into this work, we actually grow and evolve, moving to a kinder, deeper dimension of self-awareness. We become gentle but honest students of our interior life.

This needs to become an intentional practice because ego-deflating work isn't something that we happily take on, or that just happens naturally. In fact, we fight it! Not many of us wake up in the morning, wanting to spend the day uncovering what is buried inside. That's why it has been hiding all of these years! And yet keeping it hidden is the only way it can continue to have an influence on us; as soon as we become aware of it and shine the light on it, it loses its power. The price of admission to step into transformation is the willingness to leave the past behind, and to let go of the load we have been dragging around like oversized baggage.

So what do we use as our wake-up call? How do we become aware of what is unconsciously happening under the cloak of the shadow? How do we peek behind the mask of the ego? Moments of having our buttons pushed are golden opportunities to do the healing work. Our projections can help shine a light on the ego's antics, and uncover previously unconscious blue pill shadowy behavior. As Richard Rohr puts it, "Our wounds are God's hiding place and hold our greatest gifts."

Iyanla Vanzant tells us to bless people that get on our nerves. The reason for that is because, with precise accuracy, they can zero in and help to pinpoint places within us that are in need of healing. Being grateful for the person who pushes our buttons is a large part of the healing process. That is because they are helping to unveil something we often don't see. It is usually an unconscious pattern of some kind that is being triggered, and so those closest to us can mirror our healing needs in a wonderful way. Being grateful for the triggering moment opens up great possibility for healing.

There is a story told about an old sailor who was never seen without a smoking cigar perpetually perched out of the side of his mouth. He had a parrot that developed a very bad cough and the sailor worriedly took the bird to a vet to find out what was wrong with his beloved pet. The vet listened to the parrot, examined the bird and then turned to the sailor and said, "There is nothing wrong with your pet." The sailor sighed in relief. Then the doctor added, "He is imitating you!"

Those around us can point the way to our own healing by holding up a mirror that reflects what we aren't seeing within ourselves. Our button pushers provide endless red pill healing opportunities.

Red Pill Practice

1. When have you had your buttons pushed?

2. Describe a time when you were triggered by a situation that mirrored a healing opportunity for you.

3. What was the pain point that this "button" pushed?

Chapter 10 Believing is Seeing

"Why, sometimes I've believed as many as six impossible things before breakfast." (Spoken by the Red Queen) Lewis Carroll

In the 1980's, psychologist Dr. Ellen Langer brought together an aging group of men, who had been in the prime of their life in the 1950s, to spend five days at a retreat center. The center was decorated to look and feel exactly as it would have in the '50s. Issues of *Life* magazine and *The Saturday Evening Post* were spread out on the tables, and all of the furniture was the same as it was then, including a black-and-white TV. The men watched shows popular in the '50s and listened to Perry Como and Nat King Cole on the radio. They watched news programs featuring Walter Cronkite and others from that era.

They also discussed events of the past as if they were current: Fidel Castro's rise in power, Nikita Khrushchev's visit to the US, the feats of Mickey Mantle and Floyd Patterson. It was all designed to help the men imagine and feel as though they were 25 years younger, to the point that they could actually believe it to be true.

After five days, the researchers measured several markers – height, weight, flexibility, eyesight, hearing, memory – and compared them to the measurements taken before the retreat. Their scores improved by sixty-three percent. They even grew in height as their spines straightened. The men literally became younger in those five days. They were able to turn on the circuits in their brains that reminded them of who they had been twenty-five years earlier, and their body chemistry responded. They changed their minds and their bodies followed suit. Despite falling under the bloated nothingness umbrella, beliefs are surprisingly powerful.

The Placebo Effect

"The confidence people have in their beliefs is not a measure of the quality of evidence but of the coherence of the story that the mind has managed to construct." Daniel Kahneman

The power of belief has been well documented in the science field for many years. During scientific study testing a drug's efficacy, researchers will use two groups. One is a research group that receives the actual drug and the other called a control group gets a placebo – some kind of inert substance like a sugar pill or saline solution. After a certain amount of time, they will test both groups and compare the results to see how efficient the drug is when measured against the placebo.

Neither group will know which they have received, and a significant percentage of people in the control group will heal because they *believe* they are receiving medication when, in fact, they are not. Interestingly, there is also the opposite effect when people who received the placebo will be convinced they are getting the real thing because even though they didn't receive it, they will get all of the side effects of the drug being tested.

This is a scientific, medical dynamic known as the placebo effect. Rather than just using it as a marker to test a drug's efficacy, I think it is equally newsworthy to study the effect itself, and the remarkable power of belief when it comes to our own healing! It is not only physical healing that can take place. Mental and emotional wellbeing can also be greatly affected by the beliefs we hold, as well as the myths and stories we accept as true.

I once read that the only thing that separates us is our beliefs. Imagine how different life might look from the various perspectives of someone who was severely abused as a child; or had a house filled with anger, rage and shame; or had cold, distant parents who never spoke to one another. Would a person who grew up in the lap of luxury see life differently than someone who was born into an inner city ghetto? What would be the unconscious beliefs that would swim in each person's psyche? What limiting beliefs are separating us, and how might those beliefs condition the way each one of us relates to life? Think about how many wars are fought because of a difference in religious, racial and political beliefs.

Some of those beliefs are pretty sticky and might show up more than one time, especially if they have been around for a while. They can grow roots and become default behavior patterns. Those blue pill behaviors seem to come out of nowhere if we are not present. But here's something to consider: Imagine that those behaviors can only show up when we have gone on autopilot. We have creative power and we create our experience of life. We can't help it; it is our nature to be creative. But – and here's the rub – what happens when we create out of this morass of limiting, false beliefs?

Conceive It, Believe It, Achieve It

> *"Whether you think you can, or you think you can't – you're right."* Henry Ford

Napoleon Hill, author of the book, *Think and Grow Rich* tells us that what we can conceive of and believe in, we can achieve. I think of it as a formula: $C + B = A$.

Conceive plus believe equals achieve.

Conceiving of something in our minds may be the important first step to seeing it come to fruition, but it is not the only step by a long shot. Believing that it is possible is an even larger hurdle that must be overcome in order to see something we have imagined actually manifest.

I can remember many times during the years of working on my doctoral degree that I would sink into a pit of "I-am-never-going-to-finish-this-and-I-don't-have-what-it-takes-and-what-was-I-even-thinking" despair. My work would come to a screeching halt and I would think there was no way I would get through to the next step. It would usually happen whenever I was struggling with a difficult course – yes, I'm talking about you, Statistics – and I would feel the weight of the enormity of the entire program.

What pulled me out of the abyss would be to return my attention to the one assignment in front of me – and complete it. Then the next, then the next, then the next. And as I successfully worked my way through each piece, the belief that I didn't have what it takes to make it to the finish line receded, until I crested the hill and scaled the wall of impossibility I had erected within my head.

To be clear, statistics never became a cakewalk for me, and I was deliriously happy the day I got a passing grade and could move on. I did see the good sense, however, in hiring a professional statistician for my doctoral research project, because – and this was news to me – there are actually people who love working with statistics. Who knew?

One such person is a man named George Dantzig. He was running late one morning and arrived at his statistics class after it was already in session. As he took his seat, he noticed two problems that had been written on the blackboard, and he hurriedly copied them down as homework. A few days later, he handed in his assignment, apologizing to the instructor for taking so long with his homework, and shared that the problems had proven to be more difficult than expected.

A couple of weeks later, on a Sunday morning at 8 am, he was awakened by someone banging on his front door. It was his professor, excited about the work he had handed in, and wanting to send it in for publication. It turns out that the two problems that were on the board were not homework, but were examples of two famous *unsolved* problems in statistics. Dantzig went on to become a mathematical scientist and professor.

Lest we get the idea that belief only affects the world of statistics, the truth is that it makes its appearance in a spectrum of ways – from believing things like we can't parallel park, fry an egg without breaking the yolk, or lose five pounds. We keep anything we are trying to achieve firmly out of our grasp when we erect a wall of impossibility.

Whether you believe you can or you believe you can't, you're right.

Red Pill Practice

1. Identify one thing in your life that you want to achieve but have erected a wall of impossibility.

2. What is one small step you can take that can help you begin to scale that wall?

3. In what ways have you noticed the Placebo Effect or self-fulfilling prophecies operating in your life?

Chapter 11 A Universe Made of Stories

"That's my story and it's sticking to me." Dennis Merritt Jones

When beliefs are deeply ingrained, they can turn into our life story. If I have a belief that life is always a struggle – even though that may not be the truth – that is what my experience of life will be. Whatever is happening around me will be filtered through the lens of "struggle," and therefore it will confirm the belief for me even when it isn't true.

Believing something is impossible seals the deal, and sets the goal or intention firmly out of my reach. So if I have a desire to be successful, I might do all the "right things" by trying to envision success, setting an intention for success, journaling about success, creating a vision board and looking at it three times a day. If, at the same time, I secretly believe it is impossible for me, the belief wins every time, hands down.

I might find that I can't lose weight or that I always seem to blurt out the wrong thing at the wrong time, or that I am engaging in addictive behavior that I can't seem to stop. Every time I get close to being successful, triumph eludes me in some way. I might see some progress but then self-sabotage takes over, and stops me from going any further than I secretly believe that I can go. Self-defeating behavior swoops in with the proverbial monkey wrench, tosses it in, and we find ourselves thinking, "I can't *believe* I am back here again" while cuddling up with Ben and Jerry. As New Thought minister Chris Michaels puts it, "My self-destruct button had been pushed so many times, the lettering on it had worn off."

Noticing these self-sabotaging patterns can be the outer clues showing us what the hidden belief might be, and we can use those clues to consciously awaken. As Marlise Karlin, a researcher in the mind-body field, notes: "It isn't what you intellectually know that influences your health and well-being – it's what you unconsciously believe and practice." What the mind can conceive of and the heart can truly believe, the body can ultimately achieve.

So the question becomes, "What do I truly believe about myself?" Is it "I always screw everything up" or "I can't be successful" or maybe "There is something wrong with me"? If I am seeing evidence of these kinds of stories in my life, and I am being triggered by them, it is a sure bet that I believe them at some level of my being.

Scott discovered a belief that he didn't know he had, which stemmed from a moment, as a young child, when he overheard his mother thoughtlessly remark to a neighbor over the back fence that having more than three kids was a mistake. Scott happened to be kid number four of five. And at that young, highly suggestible age, he immediately took on the belief that he himself was a mistake.

Of course, as an adult, Scott didn't go around *consciously* believing he was a mistake. But a major problem in his life was that if anyone pointed out an error he had made, especially in his work, giving him feedback in some way, those buttons got pushed pretty deeply. He was plagued with this over-reaction until he finally discovered what was behind it. It was a forgotten memory that didn't surface until he did some work to uncover it. Even though the memory of that moment had been buried for years, it was still having a significant influence on his life.

If you had asked Scott if he was upset from the feedback on an error he made because he believed that he *was* a mistake, he would likely have retorted, "That's ridiculous! I am upset because of the arrogant way my boss points out a mistake. It's got nothing to do with a belief *I* have. *He's* the problem." And he would have meant it. That is what we typically do! We assign whatever is showing up as the issue.

However, whenever we have an internal pain point, unless we do some unlearning with it, that pain is going to show up in some way in our life. Pain that is not transformed is going to be transmitted. Whether it is by beating ourselves up, projecting it onto someone else, or coping through some addictive behavior, that painful belief is going to make itself known in some way. As Parker

Palmer insightfully observes, "Violence is what happens when we don't know what else to do with our suffering." Whenever we do something hurtful or engage in addictive, self-destructive behavior, it is because at that moment we are unconscious and asleep to who we really are. If we were conscious, we would stop immediately. That is why awakening is so transformative. So we need to use those triggering moments as the clue to discovering the underlying belief. They are gold!

If I have a belief that there is something wrong with me, you can bet I will find evidence of it everywhere I look. This is a condition known as *premature cognitive commitment,* fueled by early beliefs that have been accepted as truth. Because of this phenomenon, something will happen that one person might interpret one way, but I will see it as evidence that confirms the belief that *I* hold. Whenever I come across any contradictory evidence, I will discount it because it doesn't fit in with my mental model of how life is. I will hold fast to my current belief system, and I actually will have a bias toward confirming what I already believe.

Here's the thing – if something happens that disavows that belief, I won't see it. I won't notice it. I won't even entertain the thought.

We really do that.

Really!

My universe will reflect that story and I will accept it as reality. Quantum physicist David Bohm describes the reality-shaping process this way: *"Reality is what we take to be true. What we take to be true is what we believe. What we believe is based upon our perceptions. What we perceive depends on what we look for. What we look for depends on what we think. What we think depends on what we perceive. What we perceive determines what we believe. What we believe determines what we take to be true. What we take to be true is our reality."* And on and on it goes.

We are all looking through the lenses of our beliefs. Part of the human condition entails viewing life through this transparent filter of beliefs, and the biggest issue is that it is all done unconsciously. As the author Elizabeth Gilbert writes, "The truth gets screened through a thousand-layer filter composed of all of our weirdness and wonderfulness."

The perceptions we get locked into become habitual viewpoints and serve as a filter through which we view the world. You can't see without you in the view! Why? Because we are on the wrong side of our eyeballs to really see it objectively. We are looking through the filters of our beliefs – and it affects our perceptions. The way we think about life is determined by our theories and beliefs about life.

I once knew a woman who was convinced that people could not be trusted and that they were always "up to no good." No amount of talking could dissuade her from this viewpoint, and so every time she spoke to someone, she did so with suspicious eyes, and usually came away with a theory as to what was *"really* going on." Someone would say something that I would consider a rather innocuous remark. And I would watch her immediately go on high alert. Her "myth alarm" would go off, and she would be questioning what that person *really* meant by that. Her emotions would rise up – suspicion and anxiety.

Next the story would kick in. "I know that he can't be trusted so there is something more to what he just said." Then the coping strategy would be activated, and if she didn't literally leave the area, then she would at least emotionally and mentally withdraw. Finally, she would use that whole inner experience as proof that once again, she had discovered that someone was up to something and couldn't be trusted.

The two of us would both be involved in a discussion with a third person, and later if we conferred about it, I would wonder if we had even been in the same conversation. Our perspectives and viewpoints on what was actually said were wildly divergent, and we were both equally puzzled by the other's take on what happened. She would invariably find something suspicious to focus on, and therefore her experience of life was that indeed, everyone was up to no good. And who can dispute this with her? She has the internal experience as her proof. I was just as firmly convinced that nothing more was going on, and that she was misinterpreting what was said.

So... which one of us was "right" and had the correct view? Although we both would have liked to claim the title, the truth is – neither. The experience was perceived through each of our ego-agendas, and that precipitated what each of us saw. We made meaning out of it depending on the subjective filter that we looked through.

What I am describing is not an anomaly. We all participate in this!

How can we overcome this massive chasm of misperception? It all comes down to the red pill practice of *compassionate self-inquiry* and we have to dig a little to get there. You can't just plaster a positive thought over a limiting belief and expect change in your life. That is like putting a bandage over a festering wound. Healing won't happen unless we address the underlying injury.

We treat the wound by uncovering the limiting belief, shining the light of day on it, questioning it, bathing it in self-compassion and then taking authentic action that demonstrates the antidote. Just because I have a thought doesn't mean it's true! Questioning assumptions, and becoming aware of these hidden habitual beliefs, creates the freedom to make new choices that have the potential to create new, life-affirming patterns.

When we let go of a limiting belief, it is actually a liberation from a false story that has been manufactured by the mind and that has kept us captive in a prison of our own making. Alexander Loyd, in the book, *The Healing Code,* refers to these beliefs as radio stations broadcasting propaganda about ourselves constantly into our own ears.

What a relief to be free of that.

As we uncover the limiting beliefs we have bought into since childhood, we become aware of the myths that we have made up about how our lives are. We are narrative beings, and stories help us to make sense of and find meaning in what happens in our lives. The mind acts as commentator, doing the play-by-play on all the current action. And the narrative it gives is often critical. "This is boring." "What on earth is she wearing?" "There's my boss, I'd better get back to work." "I should have gone to bed earlier." "I'm starving. Two more hours till lunch, I'll never make it." "When will this be over?" "I'm late again!" "It's cold in here…" on and on and on. All of this is happening under the surface like an earworm, negatively impacting our internal state.

Believing the stories that are made up around whatever is currently happening is what causes us the problem, rather than what is actually going on. In truth, the situation is neutral, it is the story that has the juice. So what story are you making up about your life right now? Because the good news is that there is a way to change that story.

When you were a child – say around the age of two – you most likely thought your parents were physically invincible. I have watched my little grandson at that age playing with his daddy on the floor and leaping into his waiting arms with the confidence of a seasoned mosh pit diver, trusting that dad can easily handle a hurtling child flying through the air. When you were his age, you probably thought that too. Unless you are a descendent of Superman or Wonder Woman, chances are good that you probably don't still believe your parents are physically invincible.

We *can* change our beliefs.

Then there's Santa Claus. Many of us who celebrate Christmas grew up believing that a jolly old dude with a flying sleigh delivered gifts to children all over the world in one night. The time came in our cognitive development where we started poking holes in the story and seeing it for what it was – spoiler alert, if you still believe in Santa, skip to the next paragraph – a mythological tale based on a kindly Greek bishop from the early first century. But it was really Mom or Dad feverishly putting together bicycles and dollhouses at midnight on Christmas Eve.

These are examples of faulty beliefs eventually being replaced when our developmental reasoning skills helped us to see they weren't true. The light turns on and we recognize them as untrue. When we really see through them, we easily let them go, dumping them like a hot potato. They are simply no longer part of our belief system.

We have the ability to use that same internal system to bust other faulty beliefs, weaken and dissolve limiting patterns of behavior, and replace them with empowering, life-affirming ones. The bottom line is that we won't live an awakened life if we continue being unconsciously run by hidden beliefs.

There is an ancient story told of a Sufi trickster named Nasrudin. One day he happened upon a man who was crying. When he asked him what was the matter, the man showed him a small bag and said, "Everything I own is in this little bag. I am so poor!" And he wailed on.

Nasrudin grabbed the bag and ran with it until he was out of sight. Then he set the bag down in plain view, knowing that the man was headed in his direction, and hid behind a rock.

When the man discovered the bag, he shouted for joy, thanking God for its return. At this point, Nasrudin sprang up from behind the rock and asked the man, "How is it that this bag once made you weep, and now makes you jump for joy?"

By changing the filter that we see through, we can transform our life.

Sow a Habit, Reap a Destiny

Quick quiz: What do the following people have in common? Ralph Waldo Emerson, Lao Tzu, Frank Outlaw, Charles Reade, Steven Covey, Buddha and Margaret Thatcher's dad.

Give up?

Every one of these individuals has been credited with the following quote:

"Watch your thoughts. They become words. Watch your words. They become deeds. Watch your deeds. They become habits. Watch your habits. They become character. Character is everything."

Whoever said it – maybe they all did – it bears close examination. If we continue to engage in conditioned, habitual behavior run by the same automatic patterns and fueled by the same thoughts and emotions that are typically entertained, then the future looks pretty much the same as the past. Is the character we are sowing truly who we have come here to be?

Give up the idea that your life can't change or that the future is going to be the very same as the past, because the now moment is the doorway to healing. It entails the changing of your beliefs. Since they have been hiding under the surface of our conscious awareness, before we can change the beliefs, first we need to identify them. One way to become aware of what our internal state is, and to shine the light of awareness onto what is happening within us, is through our judgments toward others.

Red Pill Practice

We have a golden awakening opportunity whenever we have a triggering moment – first, to help uncover a typically hidden, unconscious dynamic, and then to do the loving, compassionate integration work.

When you're triggered – for example, someone says something to you that stimulates a reaction and your button is pushed, take some time to get heart-centered (Red Pill Practice at the end of Chapter 7), then go through these steps:

1. Briefly write down what happened in as few words as possible. We don't want to go into detail or stay stuck in the story.

2. Identify the feelings that arose in the triggering moment.

3. Find a time earlier in life when you felt the same way and write a brief description of the incident.

4. Discover what the belief you took on at that young age might be.

Chapter 12 Judgment Schmudgment

"Judgments prevent us from seeing the good that lies beyond appearances." Wayne Dyer

My friend Gail was going through a very rough period. Her brother had died a few weeks earlier, and her family had become fractured in the aftermath of his death. She was teaching a college class in addition to a full-time job, and she was not enjoying it. In fact, she found herself often being very stressed out. To make matters worse, her hair was driving her crazy. It was long and wild and she was thinking of getting it cut. On this particular day, she was having a very bad hair day, and it was full of static electricity as she was starting the class.

It was Gail's habit to begin each class session by reading aloud something inspiring or uplifting before they got to the serious business of the day's lesson. She was preparing to read a Mary Oliver poem to the class when she saw that the students had teacher evaluations to fill out. She couldn't be in the room while they completed them, so she set down her books and left.

While she waited, she had ten minutes to worry about those evaluations. Her heart was not into teaching right now and she was sure the students could feel that, so she suspected that the class would not evaluate her positively. When the students were done completing the evaluations, Gail went back into the classroom and picked up the book to read the poem aloud. As she read, she noticed that, apparently while she was out of the room, someone had put a neon green business card of a beauty salon on the lectern right in front of her line of vision, in a place that she couldn't help but see it!

When she spotted it, she was filled with anger and embarrassment. How disrespectful! How dare they comment on her hair! Ironically, she became more and more angry as she read the inspiring poem.

She looked out with narrowed eyes and saw that all the students were staring vindictively at her – a classroom full of devils. She could see the malevolent smirks on their faces. She wanted to lash out at the whole class and let them know how cruel their behavior was, but realized that would be unfair because of the imbalance of power between teacher and student. So she took a deep breath and decided to set it aside and deal with the disrespect later. She finished reading the poem and then looked around for her bookmark.

Now, where *was* that bookmark?

She knew she had *something* marking the page.

Oh. Then she remembered. The bookmark had been a business card for a new salon she wanted to try. She had set it down on the lectern before she left for the evaluations.

She looked up at the students, who were still looking at her, but they had magically transformed. No longer were they evil, cruel people. Now she saw a classroom full of innocent angels and the smirks became smiles. They were interested, curious, and ready to listen to what she had to say. Everything had changed!

Was her internal state still one of anger and embarrassment?

No! She saw the world through much kinder eyes. The amazing transformation happened when she stopped believing what her judging mind, just moments before, had been so sure had happened. Gail was having a bad hair day, felt embarrassed about her hair and so the story line that she followed made perfect sense to her. If she had been having a good hair day, she probably would have picked up the card, thought somebody must have left it behind and shrugged it off. But because of her internal state, she made up a whole story about what it meant to find a business card from a hair salon.

As Gail shared her story with me, my heart opened in compassion as I realized her experience is not an uncommon one. The judging mind can have a field day regaling us with all sorts of stories that are not true. In fact, as Wayne Dyer's teaching reminds us, judgments themselves prevent us from seeing what is beyond appearances.

Human beings are meaning-making machines! We make things mean what they mean. The judging mind sees life from a perspective that is mitigated by our internal state. We see through the lens or filter of the limiting beliefs and blue pill myths that we have taken on. And then, as Gail discovered, our experience confirms whatever it is that we are believing to be true – unless we have a red pill awareness moment, and something intervenes that helps us see it from a different perspective.

I might judge another person as a self-protective measure, in order to feel better about myself. It can be a defensive posture that shows up when I have a belief that I am unworthy in some way. What feels better than projecting that unworthiness onto someone else for temporary relief? It creates in us an ego-entertaining chance to momentarily feel superior in some way. When I believe that there is something wrong with me, it feels much better to instead focus on how there is something wrong with someone else. But when I imprison someone in my judgment, I am stuck there too! I have to stand guard at the door to stop him or her from escaping.

Magic Mirror

The author Neil Gaiman points out that ironically, "fiction is a lie that tells us true things, over and over." So, although we have a negativity bias and see the world through judgments and unconscious limiting beliefs – even if we have made up a story about what is happening that is mitigated by our internal state and may not be true – it is still valuable to pay attention to our experience, because that is when we can discover the truth that underlies the falsehoods.

Because the world mirrors back to us our internal state, we can use whatever is showing up as an extremely insightful glimpse into the mirror. The lie can point us to the truth, and it has the potential of becoming a red pill moment for us. We can gain great insight about some things that we have been hiding from ourselves.

Byron Katie was a self-described rage-a-holic who found herself in a halfway house for women with addictions. Her level of shame and guilt was so high that she slept on the floor because she didn't believe she deserved to be in a bed. But one morning, she found herself having a total awakened experience, free from the tyranny of the blue pill inner critic. She got up off the floor, went home and questioned every thought as it moved through her mind, realizing that none of the stressful thoughts were true and refusing to believe them. She became joyful as she began loving what is.

In the process of her questioning, she discovered that when she had a negative judgment about someone, it was really about herself. She found a way to neutralize judgmental thinking by writing down the disparaging statements she had been thinking about someone else, and substituting "I" for their name.

When instead we look with curiosity at what it is we are judging in another person, we can gain a clue as to what we are trying to avoid looking at within ourselves. And then we have the opportunity to do the red pill healing integration work through self-compassion.

The most potent time for an awakening moment is one in which we are triggered. This is where the mirror is most helpful. When we get our buttons pushed, it usually means that someone is mirroring something for us that we don't want to see within ourselves.

Our life circumstances mirror our internal state, and if we are filled with self-defeating, disempowering and limiting beliefs, that is what we will find being reflected back to us. As James Allen poetically puts it, "We think in secret, and it comes to pass. Environment is our looking glass." It is a sobering thought that everything I see around me reflects what is going on within me. However, as I come to terms with the dynamic that life is mirroring how I am showing up, I now find myself at a powerful choice point, and with self-awareness, I can choose anew.

During triggering moments, the goal is to catch myself looking out through the windows of misperception, then to stop, and look within for the real story. This creates a cognitive dissonance by not going down the typical road of chain-reactive thoughts, and it short-circuits the automatic conditioned behaviors tied to the past. We wake up.

But just observing it won't create lasting change. It may startle us into awakening. But if we really want to transform our lives and stay awake, then acknowledging that we may be stuck in misperception is the first step to changing the experience.

The things that trigger a reaction in me could be the steppingstones to uncovering any self-sabotaging beliefs that may be swimming under the surface of my awareness – and causing havoc in my life. Button pushers can be very valuable for me by zeroing right in on those beliefs. But what happens if I stay lost in the reflection, and think that the person doing the mirroring is the problem?

New Thought minister, Jim Lockard, explains the process this way in the context of a spiritual community: "We come together as imperfect beings (in the sense of the actualization of our potential) and we try to grow spiritually in the midst of others who mirror our imperfections back to us, triggering our negative patterns and bringing them to the surface. When we fail to see that this is, in fact, The Beloved Community unfolding AS us, we label what occurs as negative and we resist it." When I fail to see that another is acting as my mirror, I typically believe that *they* are the problem.

But as Carl Jung reminds us, "Everything that irritates us about others can lead us to an understanding of ourselves." The key is to use what is being reflected back at us as an awakening moment. We do that through the red pill practice of forgiveness.

Red Pill Practice

1. Describe a judgment you have had about another person or situation.

2. Is there a different perspective you can take? For example, if you are judging someone as being miserly, is there a way to see them through the eyes of compassion as someone who is fearful of letting go of what they have because they are afraid there isn't enough to go around?

3. How is this person a mirror for you?

Chapter 13 In-To-Me-See

"The more you know yourself, the more you forgive yourself."
Confucius

I read with great interest a fascinating account of a psychologist named Dr. Hew Len who had utilized the Hawaiian healing process of *Ho'oponopono* in his practice. The amazing result was that all of the patients in his care at a mental hospital formally deemed "criminally insane" had healed and been released. He did this without seeing any of his patients in person or creating new programs of any kind.

When asked what he had done to have such a startling success rate, he shared that he took responsibility for everything that showed up in his path, found it inside of himself and then went through a forgiveness process. As Dr. Hew Len described it, "I was simply healing the part of me that created them." He read each person's file, found the same pain within himself and took responsibility for healing it. His process was to begin by saying to his divine Self, "I love you." Then to the person he was working with he silently said, "I'm sorry" followed by "Please forgive me" and "Thank you." I recognized that what he was doing was an exercise in self-forgiveness in action. Could the process work for me?

One thing I needed to get clear on right away was that taking responsibility for something does not equal finding fault. That was an important distinction. Typically, when I thought of taking responsibility for something, the self-blame game would begin with a fruitful session of "blame-storming." All the myriad possibilities that could point the "that-was-*so*-my-fault" finger at myself would flood into my mind, and I would be frozen into inaction.

Instead, I began to consider that responsibility was simply the *ability to respond.* That had a much more useful and empowered feel to it, and in fact, it had the *opposite* effect of finding fault. Having the ability to respond meant that I could actually *do* something about the past, rather than remain stuck in ancient patterns of behavior. This does not mean that we are responsible for another's actions, just our *response* to those actions.

When the mirror reflects what we don't want to see, that is the perfect time to pay attention and do this work. Perception shifts and we actually see it differently. We begin to notice the things that are beautiful, truthful, loving and kind when we focus our energies on those things. So as we forgive ourselves, that same light of kindness now begins to radiate from within – and we see it reflected back.

To become aware of what is going on within us, we can look in the mirror and see what is being reflected. What's more, we can use those moments as what Byron Katie terms "compassionate alarm clocks."

How cool is that?

When you begin to look at life as a mirror of what is within you, it shifts your perspective from "I need to push this away," "Let me out of here," or "The world has gone crazy!" to "What is this moment teaching me?" Or, more accurately, "What is my *reaction* to this moment teaching me?" *That* is the golden moment of awareness.

Triggering moments are gold – although they probably feel more like lead. They have the potential to help uncover such a vast treasure that we want to use them to do the integrating work. However, before this work happens, we need to look squarely into the mirror and get beyond judgment as well.

I had occasion to do that one evening as I watched a news program. A local politician's corrupt actions were being exposed, and my mind was having a field day. As the story unfolded, I went to a place of judgment about his behavior, believing that he had "sold out" to corporate interests, harming people and the environment in order to line his own pockets. It smacked of corporate greed and corruption.

The inner tirade began. "He sold out!" "No thought of the people being harmed!" "They should throw away the key!"

I have a confession to make. I enjoyed being on that high horse and boy, was I riding high. Stewing in the soup of self-righteous indignation and judgment feels rather good. The ego can't get enough of that stuff.

Then I stopped mid-harangue as I realized that I was experiencing an awakening moment. My buttons were being pushed, and something was being mirrored for me – something within myself that I didn't want to see.

Sigh.

There went all of the air out of that sanctimonious balloon.

I looked back in my own life and asked the question, "When have I also sold out in some way, with callous disregard for the consequences to others around me?" As I considered this very painful line of thought and began soul searching, my memory banks seemed to overflow with an ostensibly endless supply of examples. It took my breath away as I felt that familiar sensation of sinking into the depths of guilt, shame and self-condemnation. The ego-driven urge to pounce and harshly judge the politician had boomeranged, and aimed itself straight back toward my own behavior.

Before I could mount a full-blown attack, however, it struck me. Awareness is good, but not if it is just an excuse to beat myself up. That isn't healing or helpful. What is needed is self-forgiveness. Judge it in someone else, and yes, use the mirror to find it within. But then *forgive it in myself.* Somehow I had previously missed that crucial part of the healing equation.

Archaeologist of My Past

"Become a good curator of the museum of your past." Thich Nhat Hanh

I took a moment, focused on my heart and began to feel empathy for my younger self – who had been doing the best she could with the resources she had, and whose misguided behavior had been completely driven by a need to feel worthy.

I saw clearly that all of the times I had acted in such a selfish manner were directly linked to a desire to find happiness. Suddenly my heart opened and I felt my judgment melt into complete, loving compassion toward my younger self. I saw so clearly that she was on an impossible quest to find something outside of herself that could only be found within. My heart widened, and I embraced her in forgiveness. Under a beautiful waterfall of self-forgiveness, the tears of shame shifted to ones of deep compassion, gratitude and healing.

Now my attention returned to the politician and I realized that he was doing the same thing I had been doing – trying to be happy. In his case, he was thinking that more money lining his pockets would be the answer, or that more power might do it. But he was as doomed as I was to find it outside of himself. Amazingly, I felt the same deep compassion and forgiveness for him. This practice has the effect of taming the roar of judgment and criticism toward another, letting us view them with more compassionate eyes.

In the span of five minutes, my world had changed.

The dart of condemnation that I had thrown had landed squarely in my own heart, and the forgiveness and compassion that had arisen moved outward – changing my perception of an evil villain into a fellow traveler who had lost his way.

Hang on a minute, isn't judging and condemning another's corrupt behavior actually appropriate?

Well, I still didn't agree with his actions at all, but my disagreement was coming from a clear, spacious, loving, compassionate heart. Not only that, but my response was free from the contamination of self-condemnation that had just moments before been infecting the environment.

Self-forgiveness, self-compassion – it all sounds very self-centered, doesn't it? Almost as if we are letting ourselves off the hook for bad behavior. But what are we doing really? First, we are going back into the past where we have had some sort of painful experience and we are releasing the energy around that traumatic moment. We are setting free our younger self, who has been "frozen" inside the memory.

This doesn't mean that we don't learn from what we've done and make amends. Or that we don't change destructive behavior. On the contrary, what happens when we see ourselves with loving eyes? We give the child within us the nurturing compassion needed to heal and grow. The part of us that did the hurting, the lashing out, and participated in the destructive behavior, is transformed into a much more loving, kind person who begins to experience wholeness. That is the power of this practice. There is a monumental difference between *self-corrective discernment* and condemnatory, ego-driven inner-critic tyranny.

So it begins with forgiveness and compassion. That shifts our perception to a more panoramic view as we begin seeing with wholehearted eyes. When we look with the eyes of the heart, what gets reflected back is love, compassion and caring. We see what we are putting out there.

So it stands to reason, when we don't forgive ourselves for past mistakes, when we are filled with harsh, self-condemnation – although we may believe this is an honorable way of being – the truth is that we are heaping those things onto an unsuspecting world. A person who constantly finds fault in others, thinking there is something wrong with every person they meet, invariably believes unconsciously that there is something wrong with themselves.

As Mark Twain wrote, "Nothing so needs reforming as other people's habits." It is too painful to consciously see it within ourselves, so we project it out onto others and see it "out there." It is much safer to see it in someone else than to see it inside.

When we really see that people are projecting their own self-hatred onto the world, our hearts can open in compassion as we realize this is the hell they are living in within themselves. We are beginning to embody this work when we can meet someone demonstrating mean-spirited behavior and use the power of the pause to sidestep the first impulse of judgment. It is now possible to see them with understanding and compassion.

That doesn't mean that we accept abusive treatment or become a doormat. If the person we are dealing with is dangerous, the first thing to do is to get help for our own safety. However, once we are in a safe place, now we can begin the work of self-forgiveness and compassion. Find that same behavior within yourself and forgive it!

So forgiving myself doesn't mean that I don't take responsibility for my actions. It doesn't give me license to do whatever I wish with no consequences. But it does mean being kind to myself as I take responsibility. That is the important ingredient.

When I treat myself with love and compassion, I can then lavish it onto the world. Instead of harshly judging others and projecting what I don't want to see in myself onto them, there is more room for me to become a much kinder and more caring person.

Simone was someone who judged everyone she met. Invariably, there was something wrong with *every* person who crossed her path. Frankly, it was exhausting to be around her and listen to her litany of everyone's shortcomings. I felt great sadness and empathy for her because she had effectively walled herself off from humanity.

When she started practicing self-forgiveness, I witnessed her morphing into a loving, kind person who began to notice the good in others. She had a startling realization that she had been projecting a belief in her own unworthiness onto everyone she met. Her transformation was nothing short of remarkable! And it would have been impossible without self-compassion and self-forgiveness. She gave herself what she needed, and she was now able to step outside of her self-created prison cell of judgment.

Red Pill Practice

When you find yourself judging another person, use the moment as a compassionate alarm clock:

1. Find an example from the past of the same behavior within yourself.

2. See how the behavior was an attempt to meet a need of some kind.

3. Feel empathy rise up for your earlier self.

4. Surround your younger self with self-compassion and self-forgiveness as you let go of the condemnation.

5. Return your attention to the person you originally judged, and see if your outlook has changed.

Chapter 14 But What About Me?

"Let me never fall into the vulgar mistake of dreaming that I am persecuted whenever I am contradicted." Ralph Waldo Emerson

What if I am the target of another's judgment and find that someone is projecting onto me? Although it might be tempting to smugly remind the person that their judgments are about themselves and that I am just acting as their mirror, that does not bring about healing. I heard an exchange between two people who were trying to practice the principle of the mirror – and it showed me how easy it can be to misuse these ideas.

Person #1: I am just mirroring something within yourself that you don't like.

Person #2: "Thank you, *stupid* part of me!"

Hmmm. That's not quite it.

So what do you do when you are the one being judged? It is one thing to be in a judgmental place toward another and work it out internally. It is quite another to be in the heat of the moment, having judgments hurled at you, and being able to resist flinging them back.

The Hostess With the Mostest

"Have compassion for everyone you meet. You do not know what wars are going on down there, where the spirit meets the bone." Lucinda Williams

Everything was perfect. I had done a magnificent job of hosting a retirement/going away party, with 150 guests, for a dear friend of mine. I had overseen the decorating, hired the caterer, found an excellent DJ and organized the gift table. Having completed all of the preparations, now I was going from table to table checking in with the guests, and hearing people gush over how great the party was and what a good job I had done.

It was all going so swimmingly.

Until I found myself at a small, cramped table stuck into the far corner, with a young couple sitting at it. "How is everything going?" I asked brightly.

Wrong question.

Although it had seemed like a pretty innocuous query, it unleashed a torrent of angry complaints. "This is the worst table in the place!" "We're stuck in the corner and can't see anybody else." "The food is terrible! Who catered it?" "The music sucks! When are they going to play something we can dance to?" I had inadvertently stumbled upon a hornet's nest.

I was unprepared for the strength of their reactions, and I suddenly realized that they had spent the whole evening enrolling each other in how terrible everything was. My knee-jerk reaction was to feel defensiveness rise up and have snarky rejoinders spring to my lips. Things like: "Well, maybe you should have arrived earlier and gotten a better table." "Everyone else seems to like the food." "The dance floor looks full to me." The words hovered in my mind. However, instead of saying them, I took a breath and managed to squeak out in my best compassionate communication voice, "You sound really frustrated."

Oh yes, they were frustrated all right. And furious.

As they continued unloading their anger – and they had plenty – I just kept breathing and listened. Because I was focused on my breath, I gave myself literal "breathing room," and a curious thing happened. I stopped making it be about me and feeling victimized. Instead, my heart opened as I saw what was really happening under all of the noise of judgment. I saw how disappointed they were that they didn't feel like part of the group, and that what was missing for them was a sense of belonging. They had a need to feel connected, and it was not happening. Instead of asking to be moved or join another table to be able to find that connection, this couple was projecting their hurt onto me.

I listened with a compassionate heart, and little by little, the tension was released. They stopped hurling angry criticisms and returned to the reasonable people that they were. I took that opportunity, after listening to all of their complaints, to tell them how genuinely sorry I was that this was their experience. And the amazing thing was that I actually meant it. With all my heart.

Instead of being stuck in egocentric embarrassment and shame, through the *power of the pause,* I was able to retain a self-distanced perspective that, interestingly, allowed me to stay connected to them.

I saw a softening in the woman's eyes, and she said, "It's really not your fault that we got here late. We hit terrible traffic on the way. Our babysitter bailed on us and we had to find a replacement at the last minute."

"Maybe I can see if I can find you both seats at another table?" I offered.

"No," she said, "we're okay. Thank you for listening." And she smiled.

I walked away from that table feeling shaken, but grateful that I had taken that breath that put the brakes on out-of-control reactive thinking – and hadn't followed my first impulse to counter with my own brand of cheap shots.

It was never about me. Although if I had reacted, I would have made it be about me. That is what happens when we take a judgment personally, instead of seeing that it is about something that is missing for the other person. Later I noticed the couple at the buffet, with plates piled high. And then they ended up on the dance floor, rocking the night away.

There definitely is power in the pause.

When I was immersed in the rapid-fire judgmental reaction of this couple, my first perception of them was that they were whiny, complaining and ungrateful. As I breathed and let my heart lead – instead of just snapping back at them – I saw them in a much different light. With compassion. My perception changed, and the whole experience was shifted into one of healing. How we observe something affects what we experience.

"Judge not, lest ye also be judged" is how the scripture goes. This is a brilliant psycho-spiritual statement. Very simple, but very profound. What I put out returns to me. So what do I want to send out? What do I want to share? That is what I need to give to myself.

What happens if the person who is judging me so harshly happens to be me? What if I am the one beating myself up? Doesn't that help me to change and improve myself?

Uh, no.

We can so often be our own harshest critic, and by judging ourselves, we step into an experience of separation. When we are lost in the shadow quality of unworthiness, for instance, we can feel separated and isolated in our own private prison of shame, thinking thoughts like, "I don't measure up to others," or "I am not as good as everyone else." If I believe that everyone else is judging me, why not join the crowd and look down on this part of myself too! As author and self-compassion researcher Dr. Kristin Neff writes, "We are incredibly callous when relating to our own inadequacies and we slam the door of our heart in our own face." Slamming the door of my heart in my own face. I don't know about you, but I know exactly what that feels like.

Red Pill Practice

1. Bring to mind a time in the past when someone judged you and you felt some irritation.

2. Take a moment to get heart centered (Red Pill Practice at the end of Chapter 7).

3. Consider if the judgment could have been an unskillful reaction, linked to what was missing for that person.

4. What might have been their unmet need?

The "power of the pause" can bring understanding to what is behind a judgment and let us see it through the eyes of compassion.

Chapter 15 Used Car Commercial Blues

"Whenever any kind of suffering arises, even if it's minor or subtle, recognize it is there and send it compassion." Thich Nhat Hanh

I remember a time when my karate club owner made a commercial for the dojo that was to be aired locally. I was invited to be a part of the taping, and my understanding was that I would show up in my karate uniform and be prepared to be a part of a group that was practicing kicks in the background while the owner talked about the club on camera. Sure I can do that. Piece of cake!

When I arrived prepared to practice my kicks, however, the manager called me over and said, "These are your lines."

Wait, what?

Lines! No one said anything about lines. Absolutely not!

I argued. I refused. I resisted. I battled. I whined. I protested. But to no avail.

"It is just one sentence, Jane. You can do this! We're counting on you."

Finally, even though I *truly* did not want to have anything to do with speaking lines, I very reluctantly agreed. I don't remember the exact words I was given to say but they were something about why I trained there. To me, I sounded like someone from a cheesy late-night local used car commercial that begs the use of the mute button on the TV remote.

We taped it that afternoon and I left the gym with a heavy heart, feeling upset, stressed and worried. Now I would have to actually watch the result. Weeks went by, and although I put it out of my conscious mind, it was niggling away in the background. Then one day when I walked into the reception area of the dojo, I heard the unmistakable sound of my own voice speaking and, to my horror, the manager was proudly showing a copy of it on the television in the waiting room for all of the parents to watch. I wanted to turn around and bolt out the door, except I was spotted before I could escape.

My body went into a state of traumatic shock. I couldn't believe how bad my performance was. I would be the laughingstock of the entire city over this one. I hurried into the dressing room, where I encountered some of my classmates, and the room hushed as I walked in. I hung my head in shame and didn't make eye contact with anyone.

My friend came over to me, congratulated me on the commercial and said that I had done a good job. I burst into tears and yelled "Don't lie! It's terrible!" She was taken aback by the ferocity of my reaction and tried to convince me that it really wasn't bad. But I would have none of it. Of course, my friends would say that. She reminded me that she was not the type to sugarcoat the truth and promised that if it was bad, she would tell me straight out. Besides, she assured me in all seriousness, my hair looked great in the commercial. Cold comfort.

One by one, people started complimenting me on the job I did in the commercial, and each time, I hung my head in shame and changed the subject as quickly as I could. The manager decided that I needed some help with accepting the compliments, so he made it his mission to make me watch it *every* time I came in the door. AAhhh! He stood with me holding my hand each time as we watched together.

At first, it was terrifying. I would stare with horrified eyes and find everything wrong with it. Little by little, I relaxed, and with his help, I felt safe enough to finally hold my head up and look at it objectively. With self-compassion. Instead of with the eyes of criticism and judgment.

Then interestingly, I noticed something. It really *wasn't* all that bad! In fact, it was actually pretty good! And I had to admit my hair *did* look nice. I realized through this experience how harshly I had judged myself, and how much effort it took to be able to look at something I had done through eyes of kindness and compassion.

Widening our circle of compassion – and including ourselves in it – gives us the opportunity to reconnect and, in a sense, become part of the human race again! We let ourselves out of that prison of isolation. Whether I am lost in unworthiness or self-judgment, it stems from the same sense of being disconnected. The healing remedy is to stop slamming that door. Rather, it is about opening it as wide as possible and bringing forth self-compassion.

Self-Compassion – Red Pill Practice Extraordinaire

Bette Davis declared that old age isn't for sissies. This work isn't either. It is hard work. It takes guts to walk through the fear of taking the lid off what we have been hiding from for a lifetime, and really see the contents. That is why we call on the mega power of the heart, and of self-compassion.

Bringing forth the feeling of self-compassion is deeply nourishing and healing. Here is the real gift: when we love all of ourselves, when we treat ourselves with nurturing compassion, and when "all of us" is welcome, then we stop projecting the disowned parts onto others. All parts of our divided self become integrated into a whole being.

Hidden within every moment of anguish is the potential for healing. When we stop slamming the door of our hearts in our own faces and, instead, go to the wellspring of love that the heart holds for us, we can widen our circle of compassion to bring forth an experience of integrated wholeness and awaken from the belief in separation. This opens the way for us to transform – and to step into who we have come here to be.

Self-compassion is a soothing and healing antidote to the harshness of self-loathing, isolation and separation. There is only one problem. We are so well schooled in being self-critical, judgmental and blaming that not many of us have ever been taught how to love ourselves.

Do you remember ever receiving any lessons on how to give yourself compassion? If so, you are very lucky. It was never taught in any of the schools I attended. In fact, the very opposite occurred. Some of my most painful and humiliating early memories are of being laughed at in school for saying something wrong or dumb, for being immature or not pretty enough, for having clothes not nice enough. You name it! I learned very early on how to shut down and freeze up as a form of self-protection. It was my method of finding safety for myself.

We cannot protect our hearts by having them go cold. Numbness is not an antidote. It may work to ease the pain in the short term, stopping and burying painful emotions as they arise. The problem is that it takes *all* feelings and keeps them under wraps. So perhaps there is no embarrassment – but there is also no joy. All of it gets stuck. You lose your aliveness. When you see that this is what has happened, you have already been doing it for so long that you can't remember how to unfreeze. It is a scary moment when you realize that you have become "comfortably numb," as the Pink Floyd song goes.

Addictive substances often aid in the numbness. It may work for a while. Then one day you wake up and realize you are not really living. You are not expressing love; you are just existing – running protective programming and trying to keep from getting hurt, shutting out the world with defensive postures.

When I believe I am separate, then it is natural that I would feel insecure and build up defensive postures, learning coping strategies of self-protection: blaming, needing to be right, inner criticism and judgment. When I engage in those behaviors, it reinforces the belief. To unfreeze our hearts and remove the armor, we need to use a thawing process. We do that through the power of self-compassion.

A muscle that has been unused atrophies and needs to be exercised. In the same way, we work the heart muscle by practicing compassion. Self-compassion is not self-pity or selfishness. Being compassionate with oneself actually helps to engender compassion with others. It brings about increased kindness, empathy, understanding and connection towards ourselves, and then widens the embrace to include others.

So how do we do it? The way to generate self-compassion is to shine it on places of suffering. When I uncover a limiting belief through a triggering moment, I can then go back to an earlier time in my life when I picked up that belief. So if the belief is "I am not good enough," I return to a memory from the past when I picked up that message as a child. Perhaps a parent or teacher was scolding me. Maybe I was being teased by a classmate, or being put down by a family member or friend. Whatever it is, I go back to the painful moment – and now, in my mind's eye, I surround my younger self with compassion.

First, acknowledge the suffering and the difficulty that you are experiencing. Sometimes we gloss over or try to "pray away" the pain. It is important to acknowledge that it is there, and that what you are dealing with doesn't feel good.

To assist with this, imagine a small child tearfully coming to you for comfort, telling you that someone yelled at them and that they think they are bad. If you have children or grandchildren of your own, imagine one of them coming to you in this manner. Feel your heart open to that child, and let the compassion flow from your heart. Then transfer the comfort to your younger self, the part of you that needs to be comforted.

Imagine holding your younger self in your arms. Cradle yourself in your own heart. Tell yourself how beautiful you are and how grateful you are for your younger self. Give yourself what you need. Take care of yourself the way you would care for a young child.

It is important to feel the compassion surround your younger self. Let him or her feel the love, safety, comfort and security that you, as an adult, can now provide. Really feel it. That is what you needed at that age and didn't get –

someone to comfort you and tell you how beautiful you are; that you are loved and safe, and that it's going to be okay. So lavish it on yourself now!

When the younger self feels safe, he or she will melt into your heart and integrate into your psyche. You will feel the wholeness. This is powerful beyond measure. In some cases, you've been waiting for years, decades, even half a century to feel this kind of acceptance and caring. The good news is, it is never too late!

This is a powerful practice that enlarges our capacity to feel compassion for ourselves and also for others, and we learn to give ourselves what we needed so badly in the past. When we learn to give ourselves what we need, we no longer are at the mercy of what is happening to us in our lives. That doesn't mean that we don't ask for what we need in our relationships. But our well-being doesn't hinge on someone's saying yes or no.

This is Your Brain on Compassion

There are many physiological, psychological and emotional benefits to using self-compassion. Dr. Neff reports that bringing forth feelings of compassion can reduce anxiety, depression and shame-based thinking. Research has shown that it de-activates the body's threat system and activates the body's attachment system, which calms the amygdala. Self-compassion has been shown to raise emotional intelligence and help deal with stress as it lowers cortisol levels and increases Heart Rate Variability.

Be kind to yourself. Be as kind to yourself as you would be to someone you love who was hurting. The healing balm of self-compassion is a very powerful "bully proof vest" for the blue pill inner critic.

I once read about a woman who was in therapy trying to recover from early sexual abuse in her life. She could not get past the feeling that she, at age four, should have been able to stop it. Because she did not stop it, she felt totally responsible, guilty and ashamed. No amount of arguing with the therapist about the ability of a four-year-old to stop a full-grown adult from abusing her made any difference to this woman. Consequently, her healing was at a standstill.

Until, one day, she mentioned her five-year-old daughter in one of their sessions. Immediately the therapist asked, "So, if your daughter came home from school crying, and told you that someone had done to her what happened to you as a child, would you tell her it was all her fault, and that she was bad, and should have stopped it?"

The woman was outraged, jumped up from her seat and exploded, "Of course not! How could you ever even suggest such a thi-?"

Oh.

Give yourself the same compassion you would give another.

The whole world needs self-compassion. Until we practice it, life will continue to mirror for us a place of harshness and pain. It will show us unkindness, violence, starvation, destruction of the Earth – all of it a consequence of being disconnected from our own hearts. It is the original wound from which all others spring.

There is a deep well of compassion within every one of us, and we are here to share it. As we practice, we grow in our capacity to be a source of compassion for others. This is the formula for transformation.

The world mirrors what is hidden within us, and it is through the red pill practices of self-compassion and self-forgiveness that we heal the world – from the inside out. When we do that, the distorted "funhouse-type" mirrors change and shift to a clearer reflection of what is. And we begin to perceive with the eyes of the heart. We find a whole new world of meaning opening up.

Red Pill Practice

When the inner critic shows up and you find yourself judging yourself, take a moment to get heart-centered (Red Pill Practice from the end of Chapter 7). Then bring forth a feeling of self-compassion by taking the following steps.

1. Imagine a small child tearfully coming to you for comfort, telling you that someone yelled at them and that they think they are bad.

2. Feel your heart open to that child, and let the compassion flow from your heart.

3. Transfer the comfort to your younger self, the part of you that needs to be comforted.

4. Imagine holding your younger self in your arms. Cradle yourself in your own heart.

5. Tell yourself how beautiful you are, and how grateful you are for your younger self.

Chapter 16 Authorize Yourself

"At this instant, where are the past and future? Nowhere."
Deepak Chopra

"We visited here seven years ago on our road trip," my husband, Gary, excitedly pointed out as we stopped for gas. "Do you remember?" Understand, we were not sitting and gazing at the Taj Mahal, but a Comfort Inn somewhere in the middle of Idaho.

"No. How on earth can you remember that?" I asked him with – I will admit – a slight tinge of irritation. Call it memory envy. Gary has a freakishly accurate ability for remembering such things. Like magic, he seems to immediately know his way around any new city while I continue clutching my GPS like it's my life support.

With a surprised look he said, "You don't remember?" Then he proceeded to rattle off a few more completely forgettable moments of that visit until he got to – "and then we found that *really* cool health store."

Bingo! The tumblers all lined up and I remembered.

Up until that moment, however, I was beginning to wonder if it had been a road trip he took with someone else – a "past wife experience" as he jokingly referred to it. I really *didn't* have a memory of it. I could probably have passed a lie detector test in my adamant declaration that it never happened. So how is it that our memories of that trip were so divergent?

Because memory is not reliable.

Although the brain is often compared metaphorically to a computer, the truth is that its ability to retrieve saved data is nowhere near as accurate as something stored on a hard drive. If I scan and save an image into a computer's memory and then call it up, I will see the same, exact image.

Not so with my memory retrieval. Why? Because what I remember is the story attached to the memory. My recollection is subjective and based on the emotion attached to it, along with the relevance and meaning that I assign to it. If it is my grandson's birthday, I will remember that. If it is the grocery list that I left sitting on the kitchen table, it's likely I won't.

As we know from having multiple eyewitnesses to an accident, a story changes depending upon the perspective of each observer. Who has the correct view?

Now that I had zeroed in on a memory from the trip that had emotions like excitement and delight attached to it, my memory-retrieval mechanism sharpened up considerably and I *could* remember it. The ability to recall something from the past is definitely influenced by the level of emotional intensity attached to the memory, as well as by the meaning and the story that has been created around it.

There are exceptions to this, of course – people with photographic memory, for instance. There are remarkable people who have the ability to tell you that October 17, 1954 was a Sunday and it was raining that day. You may have seen a video of a man named Stephen Wiltshire who has the amazing ability, after taking a helicopter ride over a city like New York, to touch down and then flawlessly draw the entire cityscape from memory. Although it shows me that this level of recall is a possibility, the fact is that these folks are the exception. The majority of us just don't have reliable memory.

What if I told you that this was actually a *good* thing?

I have heard from people with a photographic memory that it is really somewhat of a curse. They are plagued and bombarded with trivial information that is stored in their memory banks, and there seems to be no reprieve from it. You may have noticed that there are some memories from your past that you would rather not have in your conscious awareness, but that "helpfully" pop up regularly to remind you of the time you tripped on the carpet as you entered a swanky restaurant. Or when you discovered you had just spent the whole lunch with your prospective new boss with spinach in your teeth.

Every time we remember an incident from our past and bring it to our present awareness, we are, in essence, re-creating and updating that memory in the present moment. When re-accessing a memory, a pattern of neural activity is replayed that echoes the perception of the original event. This reconstruction isn't identical, however; it is also mixed with an awareness of the current moment. In a sense, remembering can be thought of as *creative re-imagination.*[iv]

This very act of reconsolidation of memory can change the initial remembrance. We have selective memory. We choose the facts to focus on, according to our pre-existing story of how things are in the world.

Since the memory exists only in our minds, and is not reality, we are now working with the story we made up about it. Because we are re-creating it, when calling up the memory, we are now the author of the story. And we can choose to create something that is more life-affirming! We created the narrative, so that means we can re-create it and make a new choice. We are not denying what happened; we are changing the meaning we gave to it and, therefore, transforming our relationship with that moment.

We have a great capacity to mentally re-create the past. *Counterfactual thinking*, which is imagining an alternative future, and *episodic thinking*, which is the capacity to consciously remember personally experienced events and situations, both share a common brain network involving memory, imagination and performance monitoring. In other words, remembering the past and imagining an alternative future utilize the same areas of the brain.

Interestingly, research has shown that counterfactual thinking can actually recruit and activate these areas more strongly and extensively than episodic thinking can. This means that we have lots of brainpower available to us to help imagine and create the new narrative. We form new synaptic pathways with a new memory that then becomes an independent memory over time.[v] We can actually rewrite our past, since the brain doesn't know the difference between real and imagined.

Imagine if you could take a memory from the past that has a negative emotional charge to it like the ones I have described, and change it to one that was actually life-affirming. Chances are good that the memory is not accurate, since it is subjective and based around the story we made up about it. What if we could "re-author" it, make some edits, write a new edition and re-write the ending?

What if we could return to a painful memory that contributed to our taking on a limiting belief and see it from another standpoint – the perspective of the heart? I ruminated on this idea, and I have to say the science research nerd within me got very excited.

Since it wasn't true to begin with, what if I could move beyond the narrow filter of the limiting belief and let my heart show me a wider, more spacious viewpoint? Could I then change it? Put the particle back into the wave, so to speak. Since I had penned the original and made up the meaning in the first place, why couldn't I do a re-write and make up a new "red pill" meaning? What would happen to the belief if I could change the memory?

I was about to find out.

Red Pill Practice

1. Think of an embarrassing memory from your past that still activates a feeling of shame.

2. What meaning have you made up about this experience?

3. What limiting belief have you taken on because of it?

Chapter 17 Search and Rescue

"It is by going down into the abyss that we recover the treasures of life. Where you stumble, there lies your treasure."
– Joseph Campbell

Why wasn't I connecting with these people? Why did I feel like such an outsider? I was participating in a retreat weekend of training with a group of loving, caring people. The training was excellent, the people were friendly, and I should have felt completely at ease as a part of the group. Instead, I found myself feeling isolated from everyone else. They all seemed to be having such a great time together – and here I was, quietly sitting on the sidelines watching the fun, and feeling as though I did not belong.

When I returned home from the training weekend, I became very curious about the dynamic that had shown up, and decided it was time for a "search-and-rescue" mission. I started to look into the past to see when I had felt like an outsider before. What was my earliest memory of feeling this way? What were the circumstances? Who was involved? What message did I pick up as a result?

I was transported back to my junior high school years, a time rife with painful memories. Shame researcher, Dr.

Brene Brown noted that if she ever directed a play around vulnerability, "the setting would be a middle-school cafeteria, and the characters would be our eleven-, twelve- and thirteen-year old selves."

During those impressionable years, I spent time with a teacher who gave many not-so-subtle clues that he found me immature and not very intelligent. He never overtly yelled or spoke harshly to me. But the rebuke in his eyes, the tone of his voice, the dismissiveness in his gestures toward me, gave the loud and clear message that he didn't particularly like me and that my presence in his classroom was just being tolerated. I remember always feeling like the object of his ridicule that year. Consequently, I was overly anxious and embarrassed. It affected the schoolwork I did, the contribution I made and the way I interacted with the rest of the class.

As I considered this painful time, I recognized with a jolt that the message I received from that teacher was that I was unlovable. The realization took my breath away. I found myself putting my hand over my heart in a protective fashion as the full force of those words landed. I am unlovable. That one hit home.

Believing yourself to be unlovable is a sad, harsh, isolating experience, and it often results in unconsciously inviting people into your life who can confirm it for you! And as I considered my younger years, I saw how much I had done exactly that. Always feeling as if I didn't fit in, that others didn't like me – and I certainly didn't expect them to.

I decided to do self-compassion healing work around that belief. I went back in time to that era, and in my mind's eye, I saw this teacher clearly in my mind and how he would look at me with contemptuous eyes. I heard his voice dripping with sarcasm when he spoke to me, his body language barely containing his feelings.

As I considered how difficult that school year was for me, my heart opened wide and I found myself feeling great compassion for that young girl who wanted so badly to fit in. She needed to be accepted and valued. And I realized that I could now give her what she needed. I just had to change the story. And the way to do that was by working with the memory.

Before I could make up a new story with this teacher, however, I needed to release the old one.

So I did.

I let go of the memory. What a liberating moment! I actually sensed a release in my heart that felt like an ice cube melting into warm water. I let the younger version of myself do the releasing. I saw how I had held that young girl hostage for decades, and how joyful she was to finally let it go. Releasing the memory of his behavior toward me was easy, once I let my younger self do it.

As it melted away, I suddenly grasped that what I had believed for all these years was his disdain towards me, was really his own sense of unworthiness and insecurity being projected my way. Now it was easy to re-imagine my relationship with him, and I saw him looking at me with a bemused smile, seeing so clearly in me my creativity and my gifts. I saw him being delighted and amused by it all. He became very gregarious in my memory, and treated me with kindness and respect.

I realized with a burst of joyful appreciation that I was giving myself what I had needed at that young age, and I was doing it through this teacher's eyes. Suddenly, I could feel the integration work that was taking place within me. Instead of carrying a belief that I was unlovable, I now saw how very endearing I had always been. At that point, the painful memory stopped having a negative impact on me.

I also felt as though something had been repaired from the past that had been waiting around for decades. There was something between us in our energetic fields that had now been righted. This work is done soulfully, as the person from the memory may not even be alive on the planet anymore – and yet, the repair still takes place.

A Course in Miracles tells us that the holiest spot on Earth is where an ancient hatred has become a present love. That spot includes your own heart. When the integration takes place, it is a healing that resonates throughout the energetic field in the quantum realm. An unexpected bonus that showed up was that my outlook on that entire era of my life had changed.

From this new viewing platform, the masks dropped, my perception of the past fell away and I "saw" with new eyes. I became very aware of the innocence and nobleness behind the disguise. The teacher was no longer a mean, unkind person. Instead I saw beyond the facade to the greater Authentic Self that he was. I found myself very gracefully disentangled from my former faulty perception.

I was reminded of the children's story, *The Little Soul and the Sun,* written by Neale Donald Walsh, where two little souls are having a conversation before they embark on their journey of life on Earth. Soul #1 wants to learn forgiveness this time around and Soul #2 kindly volunteers to help by providing some sort of experience that necessitates forgiveness. As the story ends, the plaintive cry from Soul #2 is to "remember who I really am" when it all happens.

Every person involved, classmates and peers, that I had previously viewed as antagonists melted into allies, friends, supporters. In fact, they became beautiful souls who had kindly agreed to hold up the mirror for me to see the belief that I had taken on of being unlovable.

Something that had been held outside of my heart melted with love, and I was no longer at the mercy of egoic self-orientation. With my perception shifting, I felt a deep integration of that period of my life. My heart had widened and there was room in it for everyone involved. The greatest gift of all was that instead of cringing with embarrassment at painful memories, I was now seeing my past with a peaceful "kindsight" and it felt whole, complete and healed.

In fact, by giving myself what I needed then – through the eyes of the person who originally helped to create the belief – was healing, in and of itself. That is how powerful we are; that is how creative we are. It is our birthright to feel lovable, to feel kindness toward ourselves, to rise up from the ashes of our past and to use them to grow into our true Self.

We all have the power to go back in time, revisit a memory, release it, and redo it, giving ourselves what we needed with self-compassion and caring. As I continued bathing myself in compassion, I asked myself, "If I was a person who believed I was lovable, what would one change be that I could make that would demonstrate that new belief?" I got the idea of looking into the bathroom mirror first thing in the morning, bed head and all, and telling myself how lovable I was. Every day for twenty-one days, I said the words to myself with joy, kindness and delight, in the same gentle way that I would speak to one of my grandchildren.

Little by little, day by day, no matter what the mirror was reflecting for me, I actually began to feel more lovable and I started to believe it. As I gained a foothold on believing I was lovable, another authentic action emerged that demonstrated an even higher level of belief. After forty years of wearing only contact lenses in public, I decided it was time to buy a pair of glasses and wear them. What did I discover from doing this? I was just as lovable wearing glasses as I was without them. New neural pathways were definitely being formed.

And interestingly, no matter where I was, I started noticing how lovable the people around me were. Since I was discovering and affirming my own lovability, I was seeing it everywhere I looked. Now that I was no longer putting out the energy of being unlovable, there was no need for anyone to mirror it back to me. The mirror could clearly reflect the beauty of a divine gaze.

On top of that, I attended a second training and found myself with the same group as before. Where I had previously experienced being such an outsider, instead I felt connected, loved and welcomed. In that nurturing environment, it was now safe for me to contribute and be a part of the group. It always had been, but because I was experiencing it through the filter of that middle-school girl who never felt she measured up, I was bound to continue having an internal experience of isolation. Even though the healing is done with a moment from the past, the restoration happens now.

The poet Walt Whitman counsels us to "dismiss whatever insults your own soul." We alone hold the key to doing that by releasing the ghosts from our past. If we are letting the past dictate who we are right now – in a way that is unhealthy and painful, using the past as confirmation of our faulty beliefs – then we are blocking our true reality from shining through.

We can rectify that by revisiting the past and re-doing it in a way that is life-affirming and gives us what we needed – but didn't get – back then. So we use triggering moments to alert us to the possibility that something painful under the surface has been touched. Then, with gentleness, kindness and compassion, we unearth it and bring it to the surface.

At that point, we surround that younger version of ourselves with compassion and caring, and we let the emotion surface as we continue giving ourselves compassion. Then we release the memory back to the time and place it came from, knowing that the story we made up around it is not true. We didn't have the developmental cognitive ability at the time to see it for what it was. And that is what we, as adults, can now change.

It is important to imagine releasing and dissolving that memory while using our senses as much as possible. See it happening, feel it happening, hear it happening: bubbles popping, ocean waves washing it away, Harry Potter-ish obliterations, ice cubes melting into warm water. Whatever it is, make it real. Allow the younger version of you to do the releasing. And do it with joy!

Then make a new choice, and redo the moment from the past with you being given what you needed but didn't get at the time. If it was understanding that you needed, see understanding shining from the person's eyes. If you weren't heard, imagine them listening with love and kindness. If you needed acceptance or compassion, let that person give those things to you and really feel it in your heart.

And then luxuriate in it. You are giving yourself the gift of having that need met after all of these years. Immerse yourself in the experience. Let the integration take place, and feel the peace and relief of finally getting what you need. With my teacher, I felt whole, at peace and immensely thankful.

The past becomes a rich opportunity to heal when we start to apply these practices to the pain points. Now, instead of wincing and stuffing down the humiliation and shame of the past, we look squarely at what happened, then with love and compassion, integrate it and heal it for good. We welcome the orphan back into the family by opening wide the arms of self-compassion. We find there is no need to be guilt ridden about the past, because the truth resides in the present. When we get to a place of seeing what the past was mirroring for us, gratitude is what naturally arises.

Every triggering moment is ripe with potential for us to look within, then discover and integrate the pain points that lurk below the surface. Whenever someone hurls a judgment toward us, leaves socks on the floor, forgets our birthday – whatever it is – if it pushes a button, it has the potential of being a "red pill moment." As author Mark Rosen points out, difficult people help to reveal the spaces inside us that need remodeling. Our button pushers are very valuable for us.

This is not about excusing abuse. This process, in no way, condones abusive, harmful, violent behavior. If you find yourself in an abusive, harmful relationship, self-compassion would say that you are valuable, you are loved and you need to get help. Some things from our past may have been exceptionally abusive and brutal, and those issues may need the deeper work of professional therapy. What we are talking about here are the pain points that we can work with, the "paper cuts" – those moments when our buttons are pushed. In fact, it is an exceptionally inappropriate over-reaction to a minor incident or under-reaction to a major one that can serve as the compassionate alarm clock, alerting us that there is something here to look at. That trigger serves as a signal for us to pay attention, since it may be connected to a hidden limiting belief or myth.

Our beliefs are strong medicine. And we create them. If we made them in the first place, then it stands to reason that we are "author-ized" to change them if that strong medicine is taking us in a direction we don't want to be going.

It is time for all of us to stop being stuck in self-hatred, believing there is something wrong with us and/or projecting our stuff on each other. We are powerful beings, more powerful than we might know. But as long as we remain in an unconscious state, being run by conditioned patterned behavior, we will just continue to create a future that is very much like the past.

Buckminster Fuller said, "You never change things by fighting the existing reality. To change something, build a new model that makes the existing model obsolete." Why not build a new structure designed to lead us to emotional freedom?

The world needs us to be who we have come here to be, and to shift our perception from one that believes in division, competition, lack and separation to one that consciously sees the Reality of One Life living in a myriad of ways and forms. We change our perception when we look with the eyes of the heart, using the quantum triad of the powers of appreciation, self-compassion and self-forgiveness. Our perception morphs into awakened seeing.

Red Pill Practice

1. Choose a triggering moment to help you become aware of something painful under the surface.

2. What was the emotion that the moment brought up?

3. When have you had an earlier experience of feeling that emotion?

4. Surround the younger version of yourself with compassion.

5. Release the memory using your senses as much as possible. Allow the younger version of you to do the releasing.

6. Redo the moment from the past and imagine being given what you needed.

7. Celebrate!

Chapter 18 Be The Change

"You must be the change that you seek." Mahatma Gandhi

Be the change that you seek.

Profound words from Gandhi, one of my personal heroes. They speak volumes.

We can't just *know* about these principles; we need to put them into practice if we want to truly transform our lives. We do that through taking concrete, authentic action.

In the past, we may have felt imprisoned by conditioned behavior patterns and been bound by the neural pathways created through repeated actions. *Now we can use that same dynamic to our advantage. We can change our behavior by creating new neural pathways and using them to lead us into awakened living.*

That is what we do when we participate in integration work – finding internal faulty beliefs, changing them to more life-affirming ones and taking authentic action that demonstrates the new belief.

Authentic action has several components that set it apart from conditioned behavior. To begin with, it is heart-inspired. Rather than just trying to figure out in our heads which action to take, we also consult the heart as to what the action ought to be.

Another aspect to consider is that any action that has the potential to change and transform our lives needs to be concrete and measurable. What would it look like if someone took a picture of you taking the action? It's not effective to choose a vague authentic action like "being kinder to myself." Although being kind to yourself is an admirable intention, what is needed is to identify a *specific* action that would demonstrate that kindness.

The authentic action needs to demonstrate the change that you are trying to create. Is it a new belief you are trying to establish? What is one authentic action you can take that would express that belief? Is it a feeling of compassion you want to bring forth and make into a habitual response? Then find an authentic action that gives you a *feeling* of compassion and do that. Is it a need you have that you want to see taken care of? Find an action that gives whatever you need to the world – and do it.

It is possible to go beyond the egoic maze of habitual, even calcified patterns, but it takes consistency. As you steadily take these kinds of meaningful, heart-centered, concrete and measurable authentic actions that demonstrate whatever it is you want to create more of in your life, new neural pathways are forged and your brain map changes.

Neuroplasticity is my new favorite word.

It refers to the brain's ability to rewire itself into new patterns of neural architecture when behavior changes. You will recall that neurons that fire together wire together, and that repeated actions become a habit – one that can turn into unconscious default conditioned behavior. The good news is that by changing the behavior with consistency, a new neural pattern gets created and the old one is pruned away. We create a new habit.

For instance, imagine if the default pattern in your life has become that your typical behavior is finding things to complain about. With consistent, deliberate intention, you can, over time, create a new behavior of looking for what is working in your life. It takes some effort to get it in gear, but once those neural pathways start to form, it gets easier and feels more natural. It is like learning to play a musical instrument. At first, the hand movements feel unfamiliar and difficult. As you practice, things start to feel less clumsy and eventually – hey, look at you – you've become a virtuoso!

We can use this same process to become kinder, more appreciative, more compassionate, more forgiving. Whatever you want to see more of in your life, you can bring it forth by consistently practicing it.

It takes about twenty-one days to create a new habit and generate new neural pathways, as some very interesting research from NASA has demonstrated. During the training of a group of astronauts, scientists wanted to subject them to the rigors of space travel to see how they fared. In space there is no orientation of up or down. One of the training experiments they did was to have the astronauts wearing concave glasses that made everything look as if it was upside down.

In twenty-one to twenty-four days, *the brains of the astronauts adapted to the change in input, and while wearing the glasses, they could see everything right-side up*. A second group was asked to remove the glasses at day fifteen and put them back on. They still needed twenty-one to twenty-four consecutive days of consistent input for the switch to occur.

If you "fall off the wagon" and find yourself sleepwalking again, then give yourself a good healthy dose of compassion and mix it in with some forgiveness, then climb back into the saddle, rub the sleep out of your eyes and carry on. It takes some work to prune away the current neural architecture and create new habits.

After returning from a few weeks in space, the astronauts from Skylab found they had to readjust to living in gravity. They would sometimes just drop things instead of setting them down since they expected them to float. Whoops. Think about times when you may have moved furniture around in a room, trying a new arrangement, but for a time, you find yourself automatically heading to where the sofa *used* to be. It takes time to re-route a habitual neurological loop.

I once read the definition of *faith* using the letters of the word as: *Feeling As If the Thing Happened.* Feel as if the thing happened! How would you feel if this was really manifesting in your life right now? Then take authentic action that brings forth that feeling. So if I want to create a more compassionate world, I start by seeing my own actions becoming more compassionate. Then I feel what it feels like to be more compassionate as I take authentic action that brings forth the felt sense of compassion. Little by little, by following this practice, I create new neural architecture that supports a compassionate way of being. It now becomes a habit and I become a more compassionate person naturally. It is now my new baseline behavior, and I begin seeing it more and more in the world around me.

After enough repetition, red pill practices can become the new norm for us. We begin to create intentional healthy, life-affirming habits rather than unconscious routines that do not support our well-being. When these tools have been integrated into our daily life, we will no longer struggle with conscious efforts. We break through our comfortable sleepwalk and cultural trance. The conditioning that used to cause us so much stress now is working in our favor as we begin to simply act out of a *new* healthier habit.

With practice, rather than rushing to judge, we become quick to appreciate. In fact, feeling gratitude becomes our go-to default emotion. Feeling self-compassion naturally arises. Forgiveness of self and others becomes our automatic practice. That happens from repeated awakened authentic action – pruning and shaping neural pathways into beautiful stretches of synaptic brain highway – that lead straight within to the deeper intelligence and wisdom of the heart.

Eventually, we find ourselves saying, "This is so natural I could do it in my sleep."

Embodying the Change

"Tell me, and I will forget. Show me, and I may remember. Involve me, and I will understand." Confucius

Unity's co-founder Charles Fillmore wrote, "We can readily see how a whole race might be caught in the meshes of its own thought emanations and through this drowsy ignorance of the man ego, remain there throughout eternity, unless a break were made in the structure and the light of a higher way let in."

The practice of embodying the change *is* the break that can let the higher way in.

Embodying means to really live something, to take it in and *be* it, not just imagine and think about it. It begins with envisioning what it is you want to create, then moves on to feeling it and then taking action to be it. See it, feel it, be it.

It starts within each one of us and then is reflected in the outer world. Authentic action is the avenue through which embodiment takes place.

When I trained in the martial arts, I started at the beginning as a white belt, and I saw myself as and believed myself to be a white belt. Little by little, I began to grow in ability, and I was behaving more and more as a yellow belt. I could perform the yellow-belt katas and movements. By the time I graded and strapped on the yellow belt, it felt right. I had begun to embody "yellow beltness." This continued for each step of the journey, all the way up to black belt.

Each step of the process was like that – envisioning the higher belt, feeling like the higher belt, taking action to embody the higher belt, then becoming it. I didn't just start at white and step into black. It took years of following this process until I got there. In the beginning, if I had strapped on a black belt, it would have meant nothing except a tie to put around my waist. I had to embody what it really represents – something much greater.

I believe we can all train to be black belts in life, mastering compassion, forgiveness and gratitude, step by step, as we take the authentic action that embodies each of them.

Red Pill Practice

What is one empowering quality that you would like to express more of in your life? To identify an authentic action that brings forth a feeling of that quality:

1. Get into a heart-centered space.

2. Ask your heart for guidance in finding an action.

3. What is a concrete, measurable action that demonstrates the quality you are trying to express? What authentic action can you take that brings forth a feeling of that quality?

4. Practice the authentic action for twenty-one days in a row.

Chapter 19 The Golden Rule

"Do as you will and harm none." Wiccan Golden Rule

I try to pay attention to things that continually show up in my conscious awareness. Mind you, I might have to notice them a few times, but eventually I clue in that there is something significant for me to look at.

If a book or a doctor or a restaurant is recommended to me more than once – if I keep coming across a teaching or a story in various guises – I will take that to be a sign that I should pay closer attention to it. There is something meaningful there for me to learn.

For that reason, things that show up in many different cultures, traditions or faiths draw my attention. It fascinates me that there are literally hundreds of Cinderella stories found throughout the world, all uniquely narrated to suit each individual culture, but with the same basic story. The reason for that is because the archetypal characters have significance for everyone's internal journey through life.

I find it interesting that the *Heroic Journey* mythology is native to all cultures in various forms. Joseph Campbell terms it "the hero with a thousand faces". Again, I believe it is because it mirrors our own spiritual journey of overcoming. I also think it is worth noting that *The Golden Rule* is found in every single faith tradition on the planet. Not just one or two of them, mind you, or even a few. Every one. That interests me. Do unto others as you would have them do unto you.

Why would this teaching be so prevalent?

I don't think that it is just because we are supposed to be nice to one another. It's good to be nice to one another. But I think the reason that this teaching shows up in every culture and faith tradition is because it is really a code for transformation. If the world is a mirror – and what we put out is reflected back in some way – then it follows that if we shift to using *the Golden Rule* as our go-to behavioral measuring tool, our experience of life ought to transform. It just stands to reason. Our actions matter, and we want them to match our intentions.

Give the World What You Need

> *"Total enlightenment can be found and expressed in the act you are doing at this moment."* Alan Cohen

One way to live *the Golden Rule* is to give the world what you need.

This is not as counter-intuitive as it appears to be at first glance. On the contrary, it is highly empowering, and it makes perfect sense to the deeper intelligence of the heart. In order to give the world something that you need, you first have to find it yourself. You certainly can't give away what you don't have. What if giving away something you need was, in fact, your purpose in life?

Imagine!

Many of us are in the search for what is ours to do in this lifetime. We may have tried to figure it out by asking ourselves what we love to do and what brings us joy. I had tried to use that method of discovering my mission for a long time. Although I could identify some things that I really loved doing – teaching, writing, speaking – it still didn't seem as though I had really hit upon it.

In my endless search for finding exactly what it was, I read yet another article[VI] on how to find your purpose in life, and it began with that exact same question, "What do you love to do?" I went on with the process and found that the second question hit a home run for me. It said that if you can't find it by asking the first question, try this one next: "As a child, what was missing for you that would have made your life so much more joyful and happier?" Well now, there is something that can hit you between the eyes.

As I considered this question, I realized that what was missing for me was a sense of compassion from my peers. It wasn't so much about my early family years, although I had my share of dysfunction from that. As Doug Krug tells us, "Ninety-eight percent of all families are dysfunctional and the other 2% are in denial." It is just part of the human condition that life on this planet has its moments of self-doubt, no matter how enlightened our parents may have been.

I thought about my needs: a need for acceptance, a need for compassion, a need for being accepted by my peers. That was definitely missing. Now, having identified what was missing for me, the next piece was to give whatever I needed to the world. That is my purpose.

And as a practice, it's a game changer.

So in my case, it is to give others acceptance and compassion. Nothing gives me more joy and happiness than doing exactly that, especially with children and youth who are around the age when I myself needed it most.

If you lacked compassion, give it away! If you lacked forgiveness, give it away! If you lacked appreciation, give it away! Return to the present moment, bring forth and broadcast a feeling of compassion, forgiveness or appreciation, then with that feeling, take authentic action that demonstrates red pill living. Guess what? We all lacked those things, unless our parents were Mary and Joseph. Hell, even if they were! It is part of the human journey. Do you see that these are the things the world lacks the most? What if every one of us missing these wonderful gifts in our lives made it our mission to give them to the world?

Sometimes the ego wants to have a grandiose purpose that saves the entire universe. There is nothing wrong with wanting to positively impact the world and make it a better place to live. However, it goes much deeper than that. What if making the world a better place can *only* happen if I make my internal state a better place to inhabit? In that case, do you see the responsibility we all bear in making this happen?

Do you want to be understood, unconditionally loved, and treated with compassion, kindness, respect, forgiveness? Then lavish those things onto the world! Begin with your own family. Do unto others because... well, if you deny others the love that you seek, then you won't find it either.

Imagine what a force for good we could be if everyone made it their personal mission and responsibility to give this world what he or she needed and didn't get. Not only do you bless the world, you bless yourself, because you give yourself what you need. When we give the world forgiveness and compassion, we give it to ourselves. And if that was missing for you as a child, then the child within you now gets what he or she needed back then. Giving stops feeling like an obligation, and shifts to actually being the Divine in action.

All of our actions that are less than loving are a consequence of disconnection, and a belief in separation. They come about because we are trying to function as isolated, encapsulated egos in a world where everything is interconnected. Change your behavior to reflect a new belief in humanity's interconnectedness, then watch the world change before your eyes.

Red Pill Practice

1. List a need that you had as a child that did not get met.

2. What is one way that you can give what you needed to the world?

Chapter 20 Resolve to Evolve

"Our world is in grave, grave trouble. But our world rests in good hands, because actually, it rests in yours." Roger Walsh

Pope Francis has referred to these times as not an era of change but rather the *change of an era*. It's all about an evolutionary change that starts in the heart. It is the evolution from an ego-driven, mind-exalted world into a transformed, heart-centered, love-based way of being. Heart and mind are connected and in alignment.

We are here to grow into who we have come here to be. Transformation is the nature of Life. It's not static. It's ever growing, ever expanding. If you are feeling this expansive urge within yourself, you are ripe for transformation. And as Pope Francis points out, this is big! It's an evolution revolution!

As Ernest Holmes put it, "Our evolution is the result of an unfolding consciousness of that which already is, and needs but to be realized to become a fact of everyday life." It's about embodying our spiritual intelligence and expressing it in the world.

This path is not for wimps. It is an art form and it takes courage to even set foot on it. This heroic journey is one of self-mastery. As it is written in the Buddhist text, the Dhammapada, "If one should conquer thousands in battle, and if another should conquer only himself, his indeed is the greatest victory."

It is a journey of the heart. There is a story told about an aging monk who was making a pilgrimage through the desert to the holy city of Jerusalem. During the day it was extremely hot, and at night it was horribly cold. There were fierce sand storms that happened during the day. About halfway through his journey, he stopped at a small inn to spend the night and to regain his strength.

As the monk was eating his meal, the innkeeper asked him how he ever intended to get all the way to Jerusalem through such miserable conditions. The monk smiled and joyfully answered, "My heart got there first, so it is easy for the rest of me to follow!"

This is the path of the heart: the journey of *wholeheartedness*. Mind and heart aligned, compassion for self and others, letting love lead. And that is a bigger shift than we might realize. But the heart is the key.

As New Thought author Michael Beckwith teaches, it isn't about making it happen; it's about making it *welcome*. Open your heart and feel the willingness to express who you really are. Spend some time in the Silence, asking your heart for the guidance that can lead you to the next step on your evolutionary path. And then follow its lead.

It is that impulse that helps us to become who we are, because it *is* who we are. We just have to get out of the way of evolution. What if evolution is merely surrendering to who we really are? Imagine that it is a letting go of the false identity – the faulty beliefs and memories of the past that are not the Truth. A surrendering of the separateness of the ego to the greater Source of Oneness.

Quit looking for a job. Start listening for a calling.

Benign Buttons

One of the ways that samurai fighters learned to do battle with each other was by hitting pressure points on the body, the sore spots. One samurai was soundly defeated in a fight and gave it all up to spend time in the wilderness, contemplating his life. Twenty years later, he once again encountered his previous opponent, who then challenged the samurai to another fight. He readily agreed, and this time, the other fighter was surprised to see that no matter how many times he hit the pressure points, there was no reaction. The samurai explained that he had spent his time during the last twenty years in contemplation, *transforming the sore spots*. They were no longer available to be triggered.

In a sense, that is the work we are learning to do: becoming aware of the sore spots within us that get triggered, getting our buttons pushed, then being curious about what is behind the reactive behavior. In discovering what that is, those sore spots lose their charge and their ability to send us over the edge. The story changes and we are empowered to transform. What used to be a trigger for us now becomes a curiosity that provides a glimpse into the conditioned, unconscious patterns and beliefs that may have been running our lives for decades. We stop sleeping through life. It is about making the unconscious conscious, and facing whatever shows up.

"Don't abide in borrowed certainty," Rumi tells us. Transformation happens when we become the change. Using the *FACE* Formula of Forgiveness, Appreciation, Compassion and Embodiment, we can truly claim our transformation and make a positive difference in the world.

It is estimated that the average human heart will beat three billion times over the course of a lifetime. (Who figures these things out?) Anyway, the point is that although this is a whole lot of beats, how many have you already had? And how many do you have left this time around?

Let's make every one count.

Red Pill Practice

1. Identify a time when you found yourself being triggered.

2. What was the need that was not being met?

3. What is one action you can take that will meet that need? For example, if it is connection that you need, what can you do that creates connection?

4. How could this action support the transformation of your sore spots?

Chapter 21 Margaret's Story

"Once we realize that we are unconsciously recreating the emotional resonance of our childhood, we have taken the first step to awakening ourselves from this dream." Michael Brown

Margaret put all of the *FACE* Red Pill Practices into effect one day when she was triggered by a situation where she worked. She had decided to try a new hairdo one morning and stepped outside the box with a very "windblown" look. It was definitely a new style for her, and she went in to work feeling very excited and somewhat apprehensive. She sat at her desk, and the first person to pass her desk was her co-worker Jeff. He looked over at her, did a double take, burst into peals of laughter and blurted out, "What happened to your hair? It looks like a tornado hit it!"

Margaret reacted immediately by feeling a surge of anger, followed by intense humiliation. Flushed with embarrassment, she jumped up from her desk and made her way to the ladies' room. Inside, she fumed and let the tears flow until she calmed down. Then she returned to her desk, but she kept a low profile for the rest of the day and hurried home as soon as she could get out the door. She thought about the whole incident and felt deep shame every time it came into her mind.

As she processed it through, Margaret realized that she had definitely overreacted to the situation. Jeff was usually very supportive of her, and not in the habit of saying things that triggered her to that extent. She realized that he was probably caught off guard, and startled into his reaction by the unexpected and uncharacteristic change in her appearance. Finally, she saw the humor in it, and she was even able to laugh about it in her mind. At the same time, she knew there was something more to this, some deeper lesson for her to learn – and that it would be beneficial for her to use the triggering moment as a compassionate alarm clock to help her awaken. Margaret recognized that this was a potential Red Pill Moment, and so she worked the practice.

She began by writing down a brief description of what happened. "I tried a new hairdo and when Jeff came by my desk, he laughed and said my hair looked messy."

Then she listed the feelings. "I felt angry, embarrassed and humiliated."

Next, she stopped, focused on her breath, imagined breathing into her heart space and thought about her loving little dog, Georgie. She immediately felt a glow of appreciation and love from her pet and let the feeling spread throughout her body. Then she thought back to an earlier time in her life when she had felt the way she had in her encounter with Jeff. As she sat in contemplation, suddenly a memory surfaced from elementary school that she had forgotten about, and she wrote a brief description.

"In the second grade, there was a boy named Donald who sat behind me in class. My mother always insisted on braiding my long hair every day, and he used to pull on the braids and laugh at the funny way they looked. I always felt angry and embarrassed, but there was no way to get away from him. That went on for the entire year, until finally I moved into a new class and away from Donald." Margaret was stunned to see the similarities between the two situations, and she saw how her buttons had been pushed by an implicit memory that had not been in her conscious awareness for decades.

Next, she asked her heart what the message was that she had picked up from her yearlong encounter with Donald, and in her mind, she immediately heard the hurtful words, "I am ugly."

Margaret gasped as the words "landed" on her heart. She felt as if someone had actually physically struck her as she reacted so strongly to those words, "I am ugly."

Suddenly, she felt her heart open to her younger self, "Little Margaret" and felt the sting of tears, as the compassion poured forth from within her for that little girl who had to put up with such relentless teasing every day.

She surrounded her earlier self with love, compassion and caring, telling her that she understood how hard that had been for her and assured her that she was loved, safe and beautiful. She kept telling her little self over and over that she was loved and she was safe. As a grandmother, Margaret imagined her own beloved granddaughter Chelsea coming to her tearfully looking for comfort, and her heart opened even wider. As she continued to embrace herself in a warm blanket of self-compassion, she was astounded at how beautifully relaxed she became, and she found herself filled with great gratitude and relief. Suddenly, this young one who had believed she was ugly, now felt valued, safe, comforted, soothed and at peace.

When Margaret was able to get to a place of self-compassion, she could then widen the scope to include the others who were involved in the formation of the belief she took on. She was suddenly able to look at them with the eyes of empathy.

She turned her attention to the young bully who had tormented her so mercilessly, and she saw a scared little boy who was ashamed of his family and his home life. She realized that tormenting her was his way of masking fear and pain while defending his own hurting heart. She felt warmth and tenderness toward him, and she imagined holding him in her embrace. Margaret actually felt a shift within herself, and a sense of a balancing of the scales, a righting of a wrong and a melting of a "hard place" within her heart. And she reveled in the deep peace.

Her compassion extended from Donald to Jeff and his outburst. As she thought about what he had said, she was suddenly seized with joyful laughter as she realized that he was right! Her hair had looked as though she'd just stepped out of a wind tunnel, and in his surprise, the words had tumbled out of his mouth before he could censor them. Margaret found herself feeling great appreciation toward him, and feeling grateful for his honesty, even if his delivery system needed work. The appreciation grew as she silently thanked him for inadvertently being a catalyst for her healing experience. In a sense, he had contributed to the depth of peace she now felt.

In this place of heart-centered gratitude, it came to her that what was missing for her in both of these incidents was a feeling of innate value. The only way that she could be hurt by either of their actions was if she was lost in a sense of unworthiness. What authentic action could she take that would give her a feeling of valuing herself?

Again she got still and listened to her heart.

As she listened for the guidance from her heart for what an appropriate action might be, she was inspired to book herself a massage. And she did so with a deep feeling of valuing herself.

One of the beautiful results of her daily practice was that as her heart opened to herself, she was overcome by a deep desire to share the compassion she was feeling with others who may be in need of feeling valued. She found an outlet for that by volunteering at the local animal shelter once a week. The happiness she found from sharing her compassionate heart with the animals as she took care of them was reflected back by their grateful eyes. This is how our life can evolve when we step into a truly awakened moment, free of any programming or conditioned behavior.

Margaret was overcome with thankfulness for the blessing that had found its way into her life.

All from having a bad hair day.

A Call to Loving Arms

Our Authentic Self is beckoning us to live an awakened life. The planet needs each one of us to move beyond a polarized ego-driven culture and rediscover the innocence of our six-year-old self. We are called to recognize that hell is of our own making, and that we have everything we need to find our way out of it. The key to the prison door rests in our hands.

We are here to be the one to make the difference in our own life, to help create a compassionate world through wholehearted living. And ultimately to stand up and boldly declare, "I AM AWAKE!"

Red Pill Practice

Whenever you find yourself in a triggering moment, beating yourself up in some way, being judged or judging another – however those emotionally painful times show up for you – remember to put the *FACE* process into practice, watch those sore spots become transformed, and step into a life of freedom and joy.

To learn more about how to do this process, visit www.theqeffect.com.

Endnotes

[i] Dispenza, Joe. *Breaking the Habit of Being Yourself: How to Lose Your Mind and Create a New One,* Carlsbad, CA: Hay House, 2012.

[ii] Loyd, Alex. *The Healing Code, 6 Minutes to Heal the Source of Your Health, Success or Relationship Issue,* Peoria, AZ: Intermedia Publishing Company Inc. 2010.

[iii] Rozman, Deborah & Childre, Doc. *Transforming Stress,* Oakland: CA: New Harbinger Publications, 2005.

[iv] http://www.human-memory.net/processes_recall.html

[v] Counterfactual thinking: an fMRI study on changing the past for a better future. Van Hoeck et al. Department of Psychology, Vrije Universiteit Brussel, Pleinlaan 2, 1050 Brussel, Belgium.

[vi] Harbula, Patrick, Four Questions to Access Your Highest Passion; Science of Mind Magazine July 2005

Acknowledgments

I stand in awe of the One Life that expresses throughout all of creation, truly grateful for Spirit's inspiration and guidance.

Thank you to my husband, partner and best friend, Gary for all of the love, encouragement and support as we journey through life together - learning, sharing and practicing these transformative principles. You are the wind beneath my wings.

Thanks to my good friend and soul sister, Rima Bonario, co-creator of The Q Process, who lives and breathes this work. I have learned immensely from your wisdom, courage and depth of intuitive insight.

I am blessed beyond measure by my supportive family members, and fellow Soul Writers. I appreciate all of my New Thought teachers, colleagues, students, congregants and friends. It is an honor to share this adventure of self-discovery with all of you.

Great gratitude goes to Tom Bird, "the book whisperer" whose gentle and wise counsel aided in the birthing of this book. Thanks to all of the editorial and creative support team - every one of you has contributed mightily to seeing the project through from introduction to endnote.

About the Author

Dr. Jane Simmons is an ordained Unity minister, and holds a doctoral degree in Theology from Holos University Graduate Seminary. Since her ordination in 1999, Jane has ministered in four Unity churches in Canada and the United States as well as serving as the Teen Ministry Coordinator for Unity Worldwide Ministries.

She developed youth and adult curriculum based on the Unity best seller **The I of the Storm**, written by her husband, Rev. Dr. Gary Simmons. She also adapted and expanded on his work, authoring **I of the Storm for Teens** She is the co-author of the beautiful, best-selling book, ***Who Have You Come Here to Be, 101 Possibilities for Contemplation***.

Jane has served as a member of adjunct faculty for both Unity Institute and Holos University. She has been a contributor to Unity's youth curriculum, as well as *Time of Family Living Curriculum* and several publications, including *Unity Magazine*. Jane has a passion for prison ministry and leads workshops on non-violence and personal transformation for incarcerated youth and adults.

Jane is the co-founder of The Q Effect and is a powerful speaker, writer, workshop facilitator and educator with a commitment to heart-centered approaches to personal transformation. She resides in Spokane, Washington with her husband and co-minister, Dr. Gary Simmons.

Find out more about The Q Effect at www.theqeffect.com.

Made in the USA
San Bernardino, CA
10 September 2018